SILENTLY,
BY NIGHT

SILENTLY, BY NIGHT

by Russell *Francis* Peterson

McGraw-Hill
Book Company

NEW YORK
TORONTO
LONDON

SILENTLY, BY NIGHT

To
Hobart Merritt Van Deusen

Preface

This is not a "scientific" book. Nor (it is hoped) is it in the "Gee whiz!" school of sensationalism. It is not a "kind" of book at all. It is a book about bats; concerning their true natures—what they are and how they react. This is in no way a "definitive" book. It is the scientist, the recognized authority in his specialized field, who must write such a volume. This is but an interim, interpretive effort; to help fill a gap and to possibly awaken an interest in these little-known animals.

My purpose has been to gather the far-flung threads of remote species, together with our own, and present them as a panoramic tapestry so we may view the entire world of bats as a whole, and not just some of the more startling aspects of a few. Although this book is admittedly of only an introductory nature, I have tried most faithfully to assure accuracy within the limits of my powers to do so. Wishing to offer as unbiased a correlation as possible, I chose, rather than follow a single acceptable authority, to include as many conclusions as possible from active workers in this field. When not able to do so, I made every effort to converge my references to traceable sources in specific areas (see Bibliography).

I have had much help from well-known authorities. Especially do I wish to thank my valued friends and colleagues, Dr. Karl F. Koopman and Hobart M. Van Deusen, of the American Museum of Natural History, New York. To Drs. Donald R. Griffin and Frederic A. Webster of Harvard and the Lincoln Laboratories of M.I.T., I am indebted for kindness and help. To Dr. William A. Wimsatt, chairman of the Department of Zoology at Cornell, I am deeply grateful for penetrating analysis and constructive suggestions. And to L. J. Evennett of Samarai, Papua, New Guinea, for many reasons, I am indebted.

Perhaps this result does not approach even a measure of their expectations. Experts in the field continually hope for an interpreter, not of infallible erudition, but one who can lucidly and simply recite what has been transmitted. We on the other hand continually seem to fail them. When in this book I lack cohesiveness; when I indulge in teleological assertion; when my drawings falter in accuracy; when I am, plainly and simply, wrong: it is not their fault. I have indeed had help. And I have a full measure of gratitude.

I have called this book *Silently, by Night*. It would seem erroneous, of course: scientists tell us that bats are actually shouting their heads off. But to you—and to me—they come quite silently, and by night.

Russell Peterson
Locust, New Jersey
1964

Contents

1

Nonmember without Portfolio

The bat is more than just an animal. He is a vision to the mind. From Man's earliest times the bat has been woven into a tapestry of fable and fact. But fancy has distorted him to grotesque proportions and fact has dwindled in our minds to mere acknowledgment of his presence. He has become less a Thing than an Idea.

For centuries the bat has been a symbol of doom and darkness. The Angel of Death, the Devil, and whoever else is particularly unsavory to our minds, is more often than not portrayed as having a bat's wings. In Gustave Doré's famous Vision of Death, a host of batlike souls follow in the wake of the Reaper. Homer fell into the same psychological trap by having the shades of the Underworld chattering like bats as they flew after Ulysses (again, on bat's wings of course). Few of us are immune. The stigma is indelible.

But however much the bat is relegated to our human world of bad dreams, sometimes he is very much with us. If, as we settle comfortably at din-

1

ner on a soft summer night, a bat blunders into our home, there is pandemonium. We rise from our chairs and thrash the air with brooms and newspapers. There is screaming and a female clutching of hair. Someone steps on the cat. Finally, the more manly among us succeeds in beating it to the floor. It is broken and smashed, taken out at last at arm's length between the thumb and index finger, and thrown upon the lawn. There is a relieved murmuring mingled with exclamations of loathing. The dreadful details are retold for many years afterward.

Does anyone ever stop to look at the creature? Not usually. And if it is touched at all it is touched most gingerly, and afterward a more than generous washing of the hands is in order. In some a true sense of terror is experienced. But with most of us it passes as an incident better forgotten. The only one who shows any interest is the cat, who, as often as not, finds the tiny corpse on the lawn and (not being bothered by poltergeists) eats it.

At happier moments one of these animals is discovered at rest. Some of us (usually the children) venture to look at it. The heady feeling of adventure is somewhat dissipated when it is found to resemble a mouse. If one simply overflows with courage and prods it, it will possibly squeak. If prodded further, it will very likely move, at which point there is a rapid movement by everyone toward the door. But at least it is discovered that it is an animal, that it squeaks, and that it "rushes at you." Sometimes it is stretched by the wings and examined, but just as often the cat is invited in. Whatever the nature of the inquiry, the bat usually gets the short end of it.

Were we able, for just a few moments, to push

aside our prejudice and hold a bat in our hands, we would fall into harmony with the arithmetic perfection of the animal, as a man grows in harmony with the suppleness and timbre of a fine fly rod. We should have cause to be amazed. For it is not his impression on the mind of man, but the bat's own identity which holds the true fascination; this delicately balanced flying machine is one of the most highly specialized mammals next to man himself. The weird tales of horror and the repugnance that have enveloped him are tamely unimaginative compared with the fantastic intricacies of his true nature.

The first shock would be the remarkable similarity between bats and human beings. The hurtling projectile one sees of a summer night, or the sharp-toothed, furry ball half-hidden under a window blind, can hardly be likened to man. But if a bat is held stretched out, it will readily be seen that the "wings" are only elongated fingers. The membrane which is attached between these fingers is quite as simple in formation as the web in a duck's foot. As a duck swims by pushing the water, the bat flies by pushing aside air. The head is often grotesquely human and is erect on the vertebral column, as in man. The breasts are reduced to two and carried exactly as in the human female. It was this fact which at first led Linnaeus to classify bats close to man and the apes. These features are apparent to more or less striking degree throughout the vast number of genera, but in nearly all the same haunting similarities are evident.

Man can quickly dissipate this seeming similarity by loudly proclaiming his obvious superiority. Here we are: you, me, Archimedes, and Sun Yatsen. And a few people in between. There are

squirrels on our lawns, and the dogs that chase them. There are bears, whales, tigers, and mice. There are cows. And there are bats. We are all here together. All of us walk or run, have some sort of hair, and our females give milk. Some of us swim. Only bats can fly.

Someone will mention birds. That is all well and good, but birds are not mammals. And flying squirrels no more actually "fly" than a small boy flies by jumping from a wall. Both go through the air, but to fly, one must go *up*. Even "flying," as such, is no great trick in nature: seeds "fly"; so do insects and fishes. I am not out to minimize the Messrs. Wright, Galileo, or our deservedly famous astronauts and cosmonauts, but none of these, nor you and I, has ever spread his own arms and soared toward the stars. Man is the greatest mammal, though not the largest (which probably pains him somewhat). But he is unique. He is Blessed. He may indeed border upon the Divine. But he is a *mammal*. A mammal is a creature with four limbs that, as I say, has hair of some sort, suckles its young, and is higher on the scale than any other living creature—or at least this is a confirmed opinion among the most advanced of mammals. And bats are mammals, no more nor less than we. I know little of the limits of man's accomplishment, but I do know that bats can fly. And I know that man, for all his lovely rockets, cannot.

There is no real "history" of the bat in its interrelationship with man. History demands continuity, and anything less than history is folklore—a sort of pseudohistory. Folklore is the term we give to fables of our ancestry. And folklore is maddeningly casual. It abounds in superstition and scatters truth down the back stairs. But it must be

said for folklore that in the bat it had a subject to
test the patience of a saint. A rat was a rat; everyone knew a rat. But here was a creature that flew
without feathers; was "blind" but could see; could
bite like a beast; that shunned the goodness of
day but held dominion over the evil of darkness.
In the language of casting directors, the bat was
a natural to be cast as the villain.

But nonetheless, the stigma placed on the bat
seems unkind. Consider the owl, who is also a
flyer by night, but who is stupid and always has
mouse on his breath; *he* came out of it all dubbed
as "wise." This doesn't seem very nice.

The folklore of antiquity is hardly less factual
than modern-day folklore. There are prevaricators
and fools in every age. Indeed, antiquity often
came much closer to the truth in natural things,
for the ancient world was far nearer to the Ele-
mental than are we. None can deny that among
the first beginnings of science were the attempts
of ancient man to interpret and explain his fellow creatures.

The bat was no less a common sight four thousand years ago than he is today. The bat swooped
low over Theocritus in the quiet meadows of
Greece, circled among the pillars of Karnak, and
flew into the palaces of the Caesars. In every age
he was there, chased, most probably, by much
the same kind of broom, but as predictable in his
habits as the fluctuations of the tides. However, although the presence of the bat was well established as a fact, his nocturnal character and habits
of seclusion kept him from any intimacy. He was
either deified or diabolized, but whatever his role
it was one of solemnity and dread. He was seldom
a friend. There is only one exception: the sensible
Chinese; the Oriental mind, so receptive to the

singular character of beauty and form, alone accepted the bat as a symbol of good luck and happiness.

The bat is often portrayed as having a dual nature. He is used by Aesop in the character of a weak liar, ready to exchange sides at the first hint of danger to himself—he is at last exposed by the powers of justice and driven from the light of day into dark places. The resulting moral seems to be that the deceitful will be given their just deserts and turned away from society.

Ancient Latin sources also cite the duality of his nature, as researched by Allen: "When the birds in council passed an edict to exile a certain one, the bat said he was a mouse; again, when a law was proclaimed against mice, he declared that he was a bird." The bat seldom enjoys the condolence of camaraderie. Enmity and distrust are his inevitable burden in folklore. Storks, according to ancient writers, placed green leaves in their nests to protect their eggs from bats, the touch of whose wings would make them sterile. Owls placed a bat's heart in their nests to protect their young from ants.

In early Egypt the bat was used as a symbol of a nursing woman, this probably from the fact that it has similar breasts. In Australia it is said that the bat was used as a sex totem by the aborigines, and that to kill a female bat would mean that one of their women would die. I found this to be true as recently as 1959 in the outback of the Northern Territory in Australia. The aborigines we found there, belonging to a tribe which came originally from the shores of the Gulf of Carpentaria near Arnhem Land, cautioned me about killing the "Wamura-mura," (a cave-dwelling bat, *Taphozous*), because it had "something to do with their women," the corpses of whom I found in open rock burials in caves. And in New Guinea, in 1956, I found the natives in Papua occasionally use bats as a totem of their tribes although in most cases they choose birds.

On what is more or less the "home ground," superstitions inherited from folklore include "blind as a bat"; that they will become inextricably tangled in a woman's hair, and that, if living in houses, they are "bad luck." There is also "going out on a bat," describing nocturnal carousing, and "batty"—having something fluttering within the cranium besides the accepted gray matter. "A bat" is still used, but rarely, for a person who shuns the day. In ancient times the same term was used in reference to debtors, who, fearing to be jailed for their indebtedness, came out only at night.

Among those peoples who accepted the bat as an actual deity were the ancient Mayans of Central America. The Bat God was one of great power and seems to have controlled the Underworld and "the Kingdom of Darkness and Death." His symbols are commonly found among the carvings on Mayan temples. Often just his head is used; at other times a human form with a bat's wings appears. Allen tells of having had submitted to him for identification some bat skulls and bones which had been found contained within a slab of stone sealed with plaster on a pagan altar in Guatemala. And only this past summer a friend of mine returned from Central America with a terra-cotta head which bore the unmistakable cleft-lip of the Vampire bat. The graphic representations of this Bat God often indicate that his temperament made him a deity not to be taken lightly. He is pictured in more than one instance biting off the heads of those who intrude upon his kingdom.

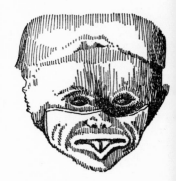

Terra cotta
Vampire mask

As a direct art form the bat is most faithfully represented by the Oriental peoples. The Chinese widely used the bat as a subject for design and ornamentation. In both jade and lacquer the bat design is often intermingled, seemingly irrelevantly, with other subjects. The reason for this seems to be its symbolic attributes of good fortune and happiness. A five-faced pendant, called a Wu-fu, is commonly worn by the Chinese. On this talisman five bats, wings outspread and facing inward, are arranged in a circle around a symbol representing the Tree of Life. This is widely used as a token of good luck, longevity, and other desirable things. The Japanese also use the bat in their designs and prints.

As far as I know, none of the very early cave drawings contained bat pictures. Prehistoric man seems to have been far more interested in more beefy subjects. Nor have I uncovered anything definite among the pre-Grecian people in Asia Minor. They seem to have been too bent on war and commerce to have much to do with inedible natural things. The Egyptians, however, as early as 2000 B.C., made paintings of bats on the walls of their tombs. The oldest known pictures are at Beni Hasan, a site of XIIth dynasty excavations.

Present-day artistic usage of the bat is limited to realistic portrayals, mostly of a scientific nature, a few radical designs by modern decorators, and, every now and then, a rash of semihumorous cartoons. Audubon made some splendid paintings of American bats, but these are little known.

One limited modern use for bat designs has been in heraldic devices. This was probably a result of an overflowing of popularity of animal representations. It seems not unlikely that blazoners simply "ran out" of noble creatures, such as the lion, deer, bear, staghound, and what not, and, in the search for variety and cleverness turned up, as a sort of last resort, the bat. Such English families as Baxter, Blake, Heyworth, Atton, and Steynings will find no humor in my hypothesis, for all have the bat figured on their coats of arms. One family, named Wakefield, seems possibly to have had a most valid reason for using the bat, if their background included any watches by night. Certain French, German, and Swiss families also use the bat as an heraldic symbol.

Man has known about the bat since his inception. The English name, bat, is generally thought to be a corruption of the Middle English "bakke," which, in turn, seems to have come from the Scandinavian. The Roman name, in Latin, was *vespertilio*, "pertaining to evening," and is still used in scientific nomenclature. The German *fledermaus*, or "flying mouse," is familiar to all of us who have ever enjoyed the delightful operetta. The French call him *chauve-souris*, which literally translated means "bald mouse," but it is interesting to note that the French also use the term architecturally to denote a sun blind. The ancient Mayan name was *zotz*, while the Chinese name for the bat is *fu*. In the South Pacific the pidgin name is *black bakkus*. But I discovered that among the most primitive people in New Guinea and Aus-

Steynings

Baxter

Martyn

tralia there seems to be no collective word for "bat" in any of their respective endemic languages; instead, each distinctive kind of bat is called by its own name, giving it a rank of individuality not unmixed with a certain dignity.

In spite of the innumerable references to this animal throughout man's history, the bat has never "belonged." He has always been, as he remains, just out of reach. That is where the trouble lies. He is not one of *us*. It is not the darkness through which he flies which hides the bat from us. It is nothing less complicated than social discrimination; just another facet of the age-old cancer. It is the old, old story. No apologist will convince us really. Prejudice has a taproot which pierces our inner being. The bat will be permitted to fly along with us, but he will not be made a member of The Club.

From an Egyptian
wall painting

2

Chauve-souris
à la meunière

Medicine is as old as man. Experiencing hurt, we have wanted healing. And there has always been someone who "knew" what was needed. Down the ages we have obediently swallowed nearly everything. We have ground down and eaten rhinoceros horn, snake's eyes, lizard's entrails, crushed beetles, and bat's brains. Huck Finn's spunk water antidote is simplicity itself compared with the intricacies of earlier prescriptions. From the witch doctor (not necessarily a fraud), through the quack and impostor, and down to our own competent medical doctors, we have always had to rely on someone—and those into whose hands we were passed had only the tools of the times with which to work. Even as to medicine "as a science," there is in reality no philosophic or practical difference between ancient and modern measures. The ancients were hardly less earnest in their desire to alleviate pain and suffering. Their methods—and methods are seen to change daily—seem bizarre to us, but, although the crudity of their efforts makes us blanch, there were as dedicated and serious minds at work in the past as there are now. The only really monumental dividing line in medicine seems to have been the advent of contrasepticity. The whole stress prior to this modern innovation was contratoxic, or against a direct poison or injury, rather than its putrefactive agencies. "Wool of bat and tongue of dog" has been altered to read "streptomycin, 15 mgs," i.e., subjugated mold or germs. But whether in the form of potions, amulets, pills, or vaccines, the will for healing is, and has always been, the Prime Mover.

It is with little surprise that we continually see, in the search by medical explorers among the shadowy outbacks of knowledge, a shadow among shadows, the phantasmal form of the bat.

Among the powers ascribed to the bat is that "if the figure of a bat is engraved on the tip of a rhinoceros horn" (Gesner) and if the prescribed prerequisites are faithfully seen to, demons will be cast out or at least warded off. Also, if a live bat's head is severed, tied in a black skin, and placed by the left arm of a person, he will not sleep until it is removed (Allen)—which I should think would be quite true, particularly in hot weather. In Syria, if a bat's head is placed in one's headgear it will prevent one from being vanquished by enemies. As a charm against evil in general, for the protection of sheep, and as a potency to insure wakefulness, a live bat is crucified, head downward, above the lintel of the door in many parts of France, Holland, and England. This cruel practice, extending over many hundreds of years, is said to be still in limited use today. In the late 1930s I found a bat nailed to a barn door in Sussex County, New Jersey, but I believe the crushed little body to have been a pathetic trophy rather than a holdover from some ancient custom.

It is not surprising to find that the bat figures often in relation to the eye. We have mentioned wakefulness. Dawson records, from an ancient manuscript, that to cure trachoma, a common eye disease in the East, "apply an ointment made of frankincense, lizard's blood, and bat's blood in equal parts." And also from Dawson, quoting from a Coptic papyrus, to cure poor vision mix "the urine of a bat, the gall of a fish, and the juice of the wild rue." Allen, quoting from Gypsy sorcery outlined by Leland, states that in Austria if one carries the left eye of a bat on his person he can be rendered invisible. An ancient Syriac book is said to have advised that "bat's heads pounded and mixed with honey" would, if properly applied, aid dimness of vision. In a similar concoction "a bat's brain or its blood mixed with buckthorn and honey," is also a remedy for poor eyesight.

In Arabia bats have been used "cooked in sesame oil" as a cure for sciatica, "cooked in oil of jasmine" for asthma, and "bat's dung, mixed with vinegar" was a cure for tumors. In France, a salve containing "adders, earthworms, stag's marrow, hog's grease, and bats," was used to cure hypochondria. In India it is said that if a wing bone from a flying fox is tied to the ankle with hair from a black cow's tail one will be assured of painless childbirth. Beyond this, boiled bat's brains are a cure for leucoma of the eyes; the fat from flying foxes prevents baldness; the ashes of burned bats will promote lactation; crushed and mixed with coconut oil, bat's wings are used as a hair wash; and bat's blood will strengthen the ear lobes. The uses would seem to be endless. But the prize recipe, from a Greco-Egyptian papyrus (Dawson) seems to be directed to young ladies in search of a man: "Take the eyes of a live bat, then set the bat free. Then take flour or wax and fashion a model of a dog. Insert the bat's left eye in the dog's left eye, the right eye in the right, pierce it through with a needle, seal it in a vase, and throw the vase down at a crossroads." There are no further directions. It can be presumed that one simply then sits and waits—and a crossroads seems as likely a spot as any.

The intricately imaginative uses just enumerated are, medically, not as wildly irrational as they may seem. Many, in the crude methods of the day, were serious attempts at research. But there are uses for bats which are neither bizarre nor unique. The efficacy of guano is known to us all, and bat guano is among the world's richest and most valuable of fertilizers. Also, certain bats are effective in the control of insects. But another use, not widely known in America but otherwise world-wide in its deployment, is the use of bats as food.

The first Proverb-Maker, that rather unbearable and mawkish old dullard who sat in some Elysian meadow grinding out platitudes, among other painful things such as "Time Flies," must have said, "Taste Varies." And he was right. But I don't like him for it.

Unicorn

Taste *does* vary. And further, circumstance and food supply and a hundred other things, all vary. We, stuffed full of A & P-ishness and prime roast beef (writers are an exception in this category), are inclined toward scorn when it comes to eating anything other than that which is generally acceptable. And what is "acceptable"? That would be difficult to say, but surely it would include most "foreign" foods such as squid, snails, and even, for lovers of Japanese provender, seaweed. All of these things are "civilized."

But we balk most firmly when certain other foods are mentioned; foods, for instance, eaten by "uncivilized" people. Grasshoppers and ants are said to be both good and nourishing. Blood mixed with curdled milk is a source of much protein. Monkeys, cooked whole and containing hair and bowel juices, are perhaps unappetizing, but nonetheless food (although I must say it is disconcerting to be handed a forearm that in every way resembles that of a tiny child!). And bats of many kinds are eaten in many ways.

I will say that all bats are edible, and I will stick to it. I will add, however, that because their own food habits are so varied certain bats are far more desirable than others. I have not tried many, but I would suspect that certain fish-eating and carnivorous bats might be somewhat "strong." But strong or not, when hunger—true hunger— is a factor, bats are a welcome food. And beyond that, bats can be quite palatable. I realize that such a statement is enough to make an epicure wall his eyes and faint—so perhaps I should say quite *reasonably* palatable.

People who eat bats are admittedly people who *need* to eat bats because other meat and other sources of protein are scarce or unobtainable. This somewhat takes the edge from my argument, but still, bats are eaten and eaten in such quantities as to be considered a staple in certain parts of the world. This is true where bats grow large enough to be more than just a morsel: the tropical regions, inhabited by the various species of giant fruit-eating bats. In Africa, India, and the East Indies, Australia and New Guinea, and on other Micronesian and Melanesian islands, bats are much sought after as food. Allen mentions that Dodsworth reports: "in the Calcutta bird and animal market several large cages were filled with bats which are bought in numbers by the Chinese, who regard them as a delicacy." I have tried at some length to find a Chinese who might shed some light on a recipe, but have thus far been unsuccessful. I have no doubt, however, that the report is a true one, for the Chinese are most fastidious and would hardly buy what could not be rendered into a delicacy.

In New Guinea, where flying foxes are a staple in some districts, the pidgin name for them is "black bakkus." I remember one of the "boys" on a recent expedition saying, "Fella belongum name black bakkus number one kai kai." Both cave and "camp," or tree-dwelling, bats are highly valued as food. These bats are entirely frugivorous, and although certain species have external scent glands strong enough to taint the flesh if carelessly handled, the meat itself though dark and rather gamy, is not unpleasant. The edible meat is more or less restricted to the well-developed dorsal and pectoral flight muscles, and the arms, though slim, can be stripped and eaten much as might a chicken wing. The legs, however, are quite impossibly thin and are hardly worth the effort. The flesh of many of the smaller insect-eating bats is often much lighter—not unlike chicken. But they, of course, are more in the hors d'œuvre line.

Methods of cooking bats differ but slightly in primitive regions, for one is most limited with only an open fire. But whether the dish is from Chambord or a native village called Waggawagga, and whether the sauce be lemon-butter or beetle juice, the recipe inevitably must begin, "take one bat..." And so, "la grande chauve-souris" must first be found and "done in." The flying fox is generally stoned, clubbed, or shot from its resting place, and is borne to the village by its soft, rubbery wings, with each man carrying only a half dozen or so, for they are quite heavy. The wings are usually cut off and the bodies—head, hair, entrails and all—are thrown on an open fire. The hair burns off, the stomach splits, and the meat (having no alternative) cooks. The somewhat overdone result is often eaten as it comes from the fire or is mixed with rice. Of course the method described above is that employed by a primitive tribe in New Guinea; in India, where curry is a blessed omnipresence, a far more palatable result can be obtained.

My own experiences were not those of gastronomic fulfillment but times of cautious experimentation. For somewhat obvious reasons I declined to partake of the native fare, although it was most unselfishly and graciously proffered. Instead, I chose privately to wash a small breast slice from each species carefully and braise it over the fire. The result: my opinion is that the larger flying foxes (*Pteropus* and *Dobsonia*) are tough, dark, and somewhat gamy, after the fashion of an old pigeon. I found the smaller fruit bats (*Rousettus* and *Nyctimene*) to be much more preferable, looking more like veal and having a more delicate flavor. Some mental reservations prevented me from enjoying the insect-eating species so I forbear to judge them.

Allen quotes Mrs. Lance Rawson, author of a famed Australian cookbook, as writing of the flying fox *Pteropus*: "... once rid of the wings and skin you will hardly know the flesh from pork ...

I cut them up, along with an onion, seasoned them with all sorts of herbs, stewed them for a couple of hours, then turned them into a pie dish and covered them with a good paste. Curried, you would not know flying fox from pork; indeed the flesh when they are in season very much resembles suckling pig."

Perhaps, had I the culinary artfulness and design, I might well have enjoyed my attempts at bat cookery. As it was, I felt I had had the experience I regarded as necessary. Not, of course, that bats are not "good eating...." It is simply that my preference leans somewhat toward roast beef. It is a pity, too, for bats (at the moment) are far less expensive.

But bats, whether served in a delicate sauce or used in a paste for the gout, are merely so much meat or medicine if their personalities and natures are cut out and thrown away. I will spare you by not quoting directly from Shylock—but a bat *has* eyes, dimensions, senses, and passions ... and is indeed warmed by the same summer. You will say that even this is degradation. And perhaps you are right.

3

Bats in Our Own Gazebo

If any intruder assaults that terminal bastion which is our home, he has far more to reckon with in the Power of Righteousness than in the force of arms. When the air is shattered by that piercing alarum, "Oh Lord, Henry, it's in the HOUSE!" there is seldom any delay in our response. The Temple has been violated. We are at a last post of defense and even with the most meek of our number our wrath becomes demoniac.

And so the broom descends. If the intruder is a bat there may be a somewhat vigorous exercise in thrust and counterthrust before the touché is made. But the result is inevitable. Right will prevail and our home will be saved.

Because it is lightly applied my point may possibly be misunderstood. However, my point is altogether serious: the home *is* a sanctuary, and violations of its sanctity should be dealt with. But I am trying hard to introduce a friend. He is an odd friend, no doubt, and somewhat withdrawn from our way of doing things. His intrusion upon your

19

privacy is always accidental, and in spite of his errors in judgment, I say he is not a bad sort. I will stick by him. My purpose here is to prevent him from being brained before his idiosyncrasies are brought to light.

There is no denying that whether as an accidental interloper making sorties over our dining table or as a colony under the peak of our gazebo, the bat is not in accord with our way of life. Birds, chipmunks, and a large assortment of daytime beasts, are as much at home near our feeding trays and lawns as are children. Even the "night shift" of raccoons, opossums, and flying squirrels are welcomed in a spirit of communal bliss. But the bat is out of it all. He is out of it all principally because he is unknown. If he were to hover over our feeding tray in full daylight; were he to alight and slowly scratch himself with a dexterous thumb, or were he to blink his little eyes and lick his chops after the fashion of our favorite dog— all of this in the light of day where he could be seen and comprehended—human society would be enraptured. But the bat, for his part, is one of the world's worst political candidates; he wouldn't deign to fly across the street for a vote.

Of the many kinds of bats throughout the world, the United States has only two zoological families represented in any numbers. Both are simply contrived in comparison with the highly intricate tropical types. The most numerous of the two kinds belong to the Family *Vespertilionidae*, or Simple-nosed bats—among the indicative characteristics of which is having an unadorned nose, and the tail completely joined all the way to its tip by an interfemoral, or "between the legs," membrane. The other type is of the Family *Molossidae*, or Free-tail bats, which also has a simple

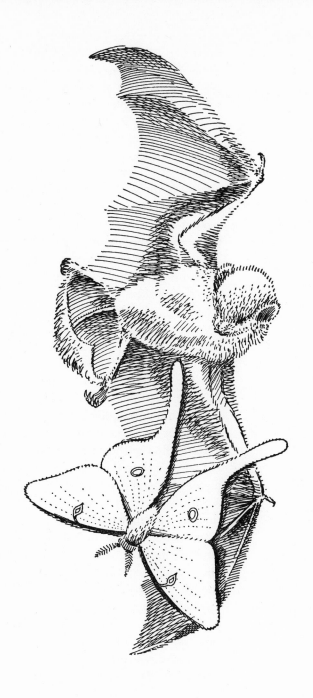

nose, but in which the membrane between the legs (which serves as do the stabilizers on the airplane) is much reduced and the tail partially free of the membrane, more or less mouse-fashion. This is the barest of outlines in separating the two; there being numerous other distinctive characters of division. There is one other family, a tropical group of bats which barely extends its range into the southernmost extremes of our country, the *Phyllostomatidae*.

Your bat, then—the one which has blundered into your home—is not necessarily of one kind. The prevalence of one type or another will depend upon the locality in which you live.

In the northeastern United States—which would seem as good a place to begin as any—the only representative group is the *Vespertilionidae*. Within this group are five principal kinds: (1) the Big Brown bat, (2) the Little Brown bat, (3) the Pipistrelle, (4) the "red" bats, and, (5) the Silver-haired bat. Again, this is an oversimplification, but these are all the layman could reasonably be expected to identify.

First, the Big Brown bat, *Eptesicus*, is the only *big* brown bat to be found in this area. And he is big only in comparison to the Little Brown bat, *Myotis*, which is (and I am loath to say it) smaller. This may sound ridiculous until you consider that it is seldom one has two bats of two kinds at one time. It is obviously silly to term one "big" and the other "little." ("*My* bat is *big* enough," you will say.) Both types are a dull brown—a true brown, in comparison to those which are brown-*ish*—but they can hardly be identified by color. The way to tell them apart is to stretch the wings to full length. If they measure as much as twelve inches it is the Big Brown, if hardly more than seven and a half inches, well, it is "probably" the Little Brown.

I say "probably" for the Pipistrelle bat, *Pipistrellus*, has much the same size and general appearance as the Little Brown, but is quite another bat entirely. In the Pipistrelle (from the Latin *pipilo*, meaning to squeak or chatter) the coloring is very definitely a yellowish-brown and the skin on the forearms and ears nearly always has a pinkish tinge; the Little Brown bat has sepia fur, black forearms and ears. Of the three types or "genera" thus far covered, the Big Brown, the Pipistrelle, and the Little Brown, only the last is broken down into numerous species, each (of the same general type) being *somewhat* different from the others, but none of these resembling anything but what it is: only another kind of Little Brown bat. Also, those we have mentioned are all colonial or cave bats, that is, as a rule they gather together in numbers, and they use either actual caves or the modern equivalent, e.g., our houses, as their homes. Most of these hibernate during the winter.

At this point, though still in the same Family —the V*espertilionidae*—we come to quite a different kind of bat indeed, the solitary or "tree" bats, which do not hibernate but fly south each winter as do many birds. These animals are in great contrast to the cave bats. Where those are for the most part dull, these are brightly colored. Where the first show fairly tall, naked ears, these have very short, rounded ears entirely covered by soft fur. And where in the first the between-the-legs membrane is without hair, these latter have that area completely covered with soft hair. The effect is that of a soft, furry, and to put it in feminine language, an almost "lovable" teddy-bear appearance. Among these is the Red bat,

Eptesicus,
the Big Brown bat

Myotis,
the Little Brown bat

Lasiurus borealis. I will unequivocally call the Red bat a beautiful animal. The male is bright yellow-orange, much like a minuscule Red fox. In this genus is found one of the not overly common examples of the sexes being of different colors. The bright orange fur of the male is in sharp contrast to the dull grayish-red of the female. The tips of the fur are white, which gives both sexes a "frosted" appearance. This bat is about the same size—a twelve-inch wingspread—as the Big Brown, but its wings are very narrow in comparison and its flight more swift and straight. Although solitary by nature, this animal is generally quite common and is addicted to chasing the moths which flutter about street and other lights and is thus prone to blunder into houses.

Another of the same genus is the Hoary bat, *Lasiurus cinereus,* so called because the "frosting" of white hairs is quite pronounced over the rich mahogany of its underfur. This is our largest and certainly America's most beautiful bat. To knowingly tread on dangerous ground I will venture to call it the "mink" among bats. The fur is soft and luxurious with muted tints of mahogany and brown, and the frosted sheen is many times more striking than that of the Silver fox. In further contrast the Hoary bat has a buff-colored throat. It is easily North America's largest bat, with a wingspread to sixteen inches. Unfortunately, it is rare. Breeding in the northern spruce forests, it is solitary and elusive, and is rarely seen except as it occasionally rests near or in houses during migratory flights.

The last of the five kinds inhabiting the northeastern states is the Silver-haired bat, *Lasionycteris noctivagans.* Here again, as in both the Red and Hoary bats, there are white hairs to give a frosted

Lasiurus borealis,
the Red bat

look to the fur. But this is a different genus, though not very different in general habits. The telltale interfemoral membrane in this case is furred only halfway from its basal extremity. In color the male is a dark sepia, seemingly black, with a generous frosting of white hairs. The female is a far lighter sepia with a much browner appearance in general. During the summer the males are solitary while the females often are gregarious. In the winter some few seem to hibernate in buildings, but far the greater number migrate south.

If this subject could for a moment be transposed into terms of baseball, we are really only saying that there are two major leagues of bats in the United States and, much smaller, a third "bush" league. Thus, if all the American League were a "family," the New York Yankees would be a "genus" belonging to that family, and the individual Yankee players, each having a different name, would each be a "species" belonging to the same team. The same would apply to the individual players in the genus called the Cleveland Indians. The Yankees and the Indians are entirely different but are related by both being in the same family or league. To a visiting European, the San Francisco Giants, because their uniforms *resemble* those of the other two, would appear to be in the same League. Needless to say, most Americans know that they are most emphatically not. Our bats, also, must be similarly organized and kept within the limits of their own leagues, teams, and players, and must as strictly be kept in compliance with the rules; otherwise there could be no "World Series," or Science.

Those we have described are virtually all the bats to be found in the northern part of the coun-

Lasiurus cinereus, the Hoary bat

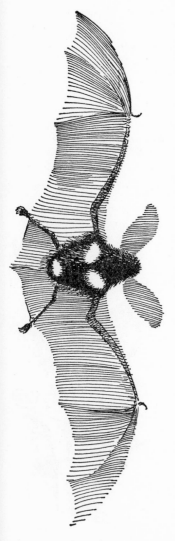

try as far west as nearly to the Rocky Mountains. The various animal identification books will show you a far greater number than I have mentioned, but you will find upon close investigation that most of the named kinds are species or even sub-species of *Myotis*. These will indeed be found to differ, one from the other, but the details are in excess of the simplification for which we strive here.

Moving southward we will find all the bats we have mentioned with the exception, during the breeding season, of the red tree bats and, extending into southern Georgia and Florida, certain species such as the Silver-haired and Little Brown bat. Among the newcomers to our list is another "little" brown bat. This is the Twilight bat, *Nycticeius*, which also superficially resembles *Myotis*, the Little Brown bat. But *Nycticeius* differs considerably in the number of teeth, in cranial and other features. *Nycticeius* has wartlike growths over the eyes, darker membranes, and a low, squat, and forward-curving *tragus* or middle-ear growth. This bat is a dweller in hollow trees and ofttimes buildings. Its flight is slow and straight compared with the sometimes convulsive flight of other smaller bats.

Rafinesque's Lump-nosed bat, *Plecotus*, is just slightly smaller than the Big Brown bat with which we are now familiar. Its prime characteristic is its extremely long ears which are joined at the base. In the hand it can hardly be mistaken for another in its territory. The Big-eared bat has cinnamon-colored fur, a long and pointed tragus, and two very conspicuous lumps on its nose. It is generally found in dry caves, mine shafts, or disused buildings, and hibernates during the winter months. It will sometimes enter houses but is by no means common.

The Yellow bat, *Dasypterus*, is a generally uncommon bat found in Florida. It can easily be confused with the Red bat but differs in having the interfemoral membrane furred to its base only, and having larger, more rounded ears, and a triangular tragus.

It is in the southern states that we first find a bat in another "league" or family. This is *Tadarida*, the Free-tailed bat. The tail, free of membrane on its posterior end, is quite different from that of any American bat not of this family. This animal is quite a frightening sight compared to the more or less small-toothed varieties we have discussed so far. If it is caught alive, it is wise to avoid the teeth, which are long and sharp. Also, *Tadarida's* mouth seems to have an unusually large gape—seemingly "the better to bite you with." The upper lip is grooved and wrinkled, and the ears are large and set grotesquely forward. In size it is somewhat medium—again, the size of the Big Brown—but it has different teeth, long, narrow wings, no tragus, and a very "leathery" appearance. It is perhaps the fastest flier among our American bats. *Tadarida* is a colonial bat and often is a great nuisance when it lives in large numbers under one's roof, for it has a characteristically musky odor. This is the genus the members of which are often called "guano bats," for it is a closely related subspecies of these which by millions occupy the caves at Carlsbad, New Mexico.

Traveling westward, into the Southwest and then to the far West, we add one more species of Free-tailed bat, and take leave of the Yellow and

Facing page: Euderma, the American Spotted bat

Tadarida, a Free-tailed bat

Twilight bats. The first of the new bats is another Free-tail, *Eumops*. It is much the same, in a general way, as *Tadarida*. Then, in the other league, the *Vespertilionidae*, or Simple-nosed bats, we come upon another big-eared bat called the Pallid bat. Except for the coloring, which is a pale and drab yellowish-brown, it is similar to Rafinesque's bat except that its very long ears are separated at the base. The Pallid bat is named *Antrozous*.

The last of the big-eared western bats is another colorful figure, *Euderma*, the Spotted bat. This is a bizarre-looking animal nearly black in color but with large white spots on each shoulder, on mid-back, and at the base of the tail. The ears are very large and have a long, rounded tragus. *Euderma* is our rarest bat.

Besides those mentioned there are, as has been said, certain members of the tropical family *Phyllostomatidae*, the South American Leaf-nosed bats, which cross the border and are periodically United States residents. Some are actually members of our fauna, such as *Macrotis*, the California Leaf-nosed bat, but as the family itself is a tropical one I would like to cover them in detail later. None of these are common.

It would be well to mention that there is no southward crossing of the northern border by "Canadian" species. Bats are essentially tropical or temperate in zonal distribution, although some, such as the Big and Little Browns and the Hoary, reach far into northern Canada.

We have now gone on at some length about the sectional distribution of bats, which is a risky business because if the country is roughly divided into quarters, there is a good chance the reader is only one-quarter interested in the whole, particularly if one has a captive bat in one hand and the

CHART I

NORTH AMERICAN BATS

SUBORDER

Microchiroptera

FAMILY	GENUS	COMMON NAME	GEN. LOCALITY IN U.S.
	Lasiurus { *cinereus*	(Hoary bat)	Entire USA
	borealis	(Red bat)	East, Central, SW
	seminola	(Seminole bat)	Florida & Gulf
	Lasionycteris	(Silver-haired bat)	Northwest, N Cent, & NE
Vespertilionidae	*Dasypterus*	(Yellow bat)	Gulf states
	Antrozous	(Pallid bat)	Far West, SW
	Euderma	(Spotted bat)	Southwest
	Plecotus	(Lump-nosed bat)	West to Kentucky
	Pipistrellus	(Pipistrelle bat)	Entire USA
	Nycticeius	(Twilight bat)	South
	Eptesicus	(Big Brown bat)	Entire USA
	Myotis	(Little Brown bat)	Entire USA
Molossidae	*Tadarida*	(Free-tailed bat)	South, Southwest
	Eumops	(California Mastiff bat)	valleys of California & Arizona
Phyllostomatidae	*Mormoops*	(Leaf-chinned bat)	South Texas
	Macrotis	(California Leaf-nosed bat)	Southern California & Arizona

(Note: There are many species and subspecies not listed; most are under *Myotis*. This omission is neither slight nor oversight. These charts are not meant to be definitive, but only as an arithmetic directional guide for the layman.)

book in the other. But we have got through it and should have a fair picture of the general distribution of bats near our home. There are, as we see, not a great number in any one section or even in the country as a whole. The total may number more or less than you had imagined, but the fact remains that each of those named is a valid entity in itself, and not in any way simply an annotated listing. These are creatures who live about you, each in his own way, but with all of the life and vibrancy of the sauciest of flicker-tailing chipmunks.

We have discussed only the kinds of bats at home. We have said nothing as yet in detail about the really important things: about their functions, their food, homes, nor much about that most pertinent of subjects, how they react to humans. Certainly it is important that we first know about kinds, for without some label of identity any information would be quite useless. For instance, saying "I have just caught a bat," is nearly as ill-considered as saying "I have just caught a snake." What *kind* of snake: a garter snake or rattlesnake? There would be quite a difference! But although knowledge about kinds of things is indeed a primary necessity in the first inquiry, such knowledge is only really useful when we can coordinate what they *are* with what they *do* and how they react.

4

A Bat
in the Hand

Perhaps, first of all, it is infinitely more to the point that we should know what to do if we should have a bat at somewhat close range, i.e., in our hand. *Don't drop it!* To many people, having a bat in the hand would be something like holding a hot coal. Certainly to drop it would seem to be the wisest thing. But we are capable of holding nearly anything; we must only be certain of *how* we hold it. With a coal we will be burnt, and with a frightened animal of any kind we will surely be bitten if the poor beast is at all capable of biting. And so, as I say, we must not drop it but must hold it another way.

The best way to hold a live bat is to grasp it behind the neck. Most probably, however, caution will lead us to hold it by the wings. But although that will prevent you from being bitten it is rather hard on the animal. A comparable situation would be for us to be suspended by our fingers; a decidedly uncomfortable prospect. But it holds true that until one learns of the nature of an animal it

is best to take the safer course. If we hold the bat
—or a mouse, or cat or dog, or nearly anything
else—by the loose fur on the back, the animal is
almost always capable of simply swinging its head
around, thus initiating the captor into some facts
about teeth.

But holding anything up by its wings is awk-
ward. At first there is a struggle on both sides. The
bat is terrified and will utter a strident chittering,
not unlike noises made by some birds in a state of
alarm. He will open his mouth quite as wide as he
is able and he will go through all the convulsions
we ourselves might if we were inescapably held
by a giant whose every action indicated he would
soon swallow us alive. But such terror can never
persist very long. You will soon see, if you hold
him quietly, that the bat will stop struggling and
shrieking. Of course, as soon as you move he will
start in all over again. However, this cannot last;
he will become tired after a time, and, having
tired, will be inclined to bargain. His conciliatory
offering will be less struggle and less indication to
bite. Ours might be to loosen our grip and perhaps cup him in our hand. Holding the animal is

something of a *fait accompli*. There is a moment
when he stops quivering long enough to contem-
plate his captor solemnly. It is not submission,
but it is a truce.

There is scarcely a more common expression
than "blind as a bat," but these black eyes are anything but blind. They are small eyes but they are
bright and alert to our every move. Blind as a bat
indeed! The teeth are much in evidence when
the animal opens its mouth, but even if we are
bitten, now that calm prevails, we may stop to
wonder what all the fuss was about. The teeth are
sharp but they are also small, and this dreadful
bite turns out to be little more than a hard pinch.
Only the Big Brown and the Free-tail bats are
capable of much more and even their bite is far
from very painful. But there is as good a chance
as not the animal will not offer to bite at all. He
will lie still and be stroked. He may grumble, in
his grating way, but that will be all.

If we stretch his wings he will probably object,
but he will generally permit it (about as we would

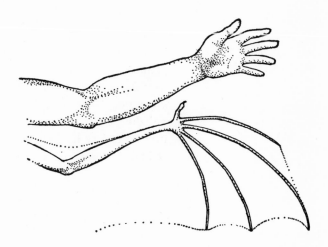

give room to a whale). The rubbery texture of the membrane has a remarkable elasticity and is surprisingly thin. The nose is rather ordinary and the ears may be oddly shaped but surely enough they are ears. The fur is amazingly soft and fine, and seems to have no "lie" or direction. The claws of the feet are sharp and the knee bends backward, quite the opposite from our own. But the most fascinating of all in a closer inspection is the one thing which separates the bat from every other animal: the "wings." They are not wings at all, at least not in the ordinary sense of feathers or aluminum stuck on the end or covering a support. They are hands. Just plain hands. Quite like our own. Every digit can be counted and recognized. The thumb, wrist, forearm, and elbow are all there. There is simply a thin web of skin between the elongated fingers. "And with just this," you may say, "he can fly?" Well, not quite. There is one more thing, but we must feel his chest and back to find it (and promptly be bitten again): the "powerhouse" of the bat—the greatly enlarged dorsal and ventral muscles without which he could scarcely get off the ground. Finally, his facilities for elimination and procreation are much the same as in man.

And with this we have a fair idea of his external characteristics. But it is time to give him a rest after the pushing and pulling and prodding. What will he do if we completely open our hand? He will do exactly as we would: go hell-for-leather away as fast as he can. But before we let him go perhaps we should see him out of the hand and on his own.

Any small cage will do. And, once having been put in it, the bat will probably not move for a moment—thinking no doubt to be roughly clos-

eted again in a moist palm. But once he realizes
he is at least temporarily free of abuse, he will
look about and take stock. He may try to fly, and
find that he cannot. He may try it again, but unlike a bird he is not likely to flutter blindly at the
bars until he falls back exhausted. Having failed,
and having learned he failed, he is more likely to
crouch quietly at the bottom of the cage or to
crawl awkwardly about seeking an exit. Soon he
may begin to clean himself. His thin red tongue
licks at his fur methodically, after the fashion of
an unhurried dog; massaging each joint of his
hand, and giving, perhaps, that final lick or two
which always seems and never quite is, final. He
may stretch his elastic wing membrane to alarm-
ing proportions, even, perhaps to putting his wing
over his head umbrellawise and pulling the membrane down as would a small boy playing with a
paper bag. Then he will stretch. He will again
continue his toilet until one might wonder how
his tongue stands it. If, then, he is offered water
from an eye dropper, he may take it or he may
not. Often he will. If he does he will lap it just
as would a dog. He may even sneeze. Finally, he
may yawn. And if after such a display of ration-
ality and homeliness you still choose to relegate
him to a Hallowe'en world of witches and spooks,
then nothing I could say further would possibly
convince you to the contrary.

It is unlikely that a newly caged bat will take
food, although certain individual bats seem to
have an almost calm attitude and will eat out of
your hand within a few hours. It usually takes at
least a day or so of coaxing, but finally they will
become more hungry than frightened. With this
bat, however, the one upon whom we have been
heaping indignities, it would be more merciful to

let him have his freedom. Later, perhaps, we will talk seriously of a longer visit. With our bat now, it is best to take him onto the lawn in the late twilight, away from predators and obstructions, so that he may get his bearings. He will sniff the air, but briefly, and then, with scarcely a sound, he will be gone. He will be discernible for only a fleeting moment, a small form swiftly spiraling upward toward the stars.

There is always the possibility that the bats in your gazebo, under your porch roof, or above your bedroom ceiling may become what is not uncommonly called (even by the vicar) "a damned nuisance." What does one do? If a remedial boarding-up will suffice, or any amicable agreement reached with the bats, that is preferable. Otherwise I would suggest the exterminator. This may sound unromantic, but an unemotional consideration by an expert is not infrequently a benefaction to both life and limb. An impassioned foray against the enemy with extension ladder, ax, and torch is more likely to break a leg or burn down the house than to discourage the bats.

We have only brushed the subject, and we have not as yet mentioned the word—but now, what about bats as pets? First of all I would like to make a definitive separation between what is a "pet" and what is simply a captive animal. I have seen nearly every wild thing, at one time or another, either dragged about by its neck or shackled to a box. I have made such captives myself when a boy. I was bitten and clawed and scratched, but I loved them all. But now I am older I would define a pet, not as something you love, but as something which loves you. It would seem, perhaps, that I am preparing to say that bats are incapable of such an emotion. I cannot. I will say that most bats I have kept were plainly captives. But I must also say I have known some who loved me. I care not at all how silly this sounds. It is true.

Bat "pets" are difficult. They are difficult in the same way as are other wild pets. They get to "love" you easily enough—but then what? Are you to keep the animal in a cage until it dies? Some do. Or are you one day to set it free? In my opinion, we must decide to do one thing or the other. Captives soon released have an excellent chance for survival. I strongly doubt that long-kept animals have much chance. After the fashion of long-kept relatives, they seem to lose the will to survive alone. If one is to have a "pet" I say one must be absolutely certain that there is a reciprocal feeling of affection, and be prepared for a long responsibility. A captive held for only a day or a week is another matter. It is one thing only: a prisoner in chains. When set free it hates all mankind. Which is as it should be. It is not love alone which leads to the destruction of wild things, but if they permit themselves this luxury it seldom fails to hasten their end. To be "wild" means to be unfettered—even by love.

All bats are not emotionally equal. Some undoubtedly make better pets than others. In order to study their reactions I have held a great number of genera for short periods of time. I kept them as long as I felt it was necessary for purposes of study. When I let them go I could offer them nothing other than their freedom. No captive is "normal," but much can be learned from them.

Rather a number of years ago I kept both Big and Little Brown bats for quite long periods. One individual I kept as a pet for over three months. I fed it meal worms—the larvae of a species of beetle which I learned bird fanciers fed to their captives with success—and the animal thrived on them. This bat was a *Myotis*, the common Little Brown bat. He was given the freedom of the house and chose to sleep in a corner of one room, hanging upside down from the ceiling molding. He flew most knowingly from room to room and went regularly to a certain table to be fed and to drink water from the inverted top of a peanut butter jar. He would come when he heard the meal-worm can opened, flying swiftly from wherever he had been hiding. This bat attacked a meal worm with considerable vigor, coming toward the proffered forceps and biting voraciously. He usually kept up a constant chittering as he ate. Others I have had stood stupidly by to be fed, like so many turkeys in the rain. One could see that this animal seemed not only to taste but almost to express satisfaction, for he would "lick his chops" and mumble inwardly. One day he failed to come to feed. A thorough search revealed no sign of him and it was presumed he had got out through some uncalked crack in the house. But months later I found his mummified body behind a blind, much as if still asleep. I never learned why he died.

I have kept Red bats from time to time. They never seemed to exhibit much of an amicable personality and seemed always to choose the path of perpetual resistance. When they were not sleeping they continually tried to escape. They would not eat. They would make no concessions. I admired them for this stand, and I let them fly away.

There is evidence that the smaller bats can live in captivity for far greater periods than the few months I have kept them. There are a number of sources which record instances of small captive bats being held for over a year. The larger fruit bats seem to live longer in confinement, certain of them being known to have reached an age of nineteen years.

I would recommend keeping bats as pets only while they serve a useful purpose, either educational or, even, for fun. But I would not recommend an emotional attachment, and for this important reason: the animal is not of our world. Like the splendid dolphins which fairly shout their intelligence at you from the sea, the bat is a unique and wonderfully contrived animal, but it cannot be a part of our lives. I do advocate a more intimate acquaintance with the creatures, both for our enlightenment and for their protection; not because there is any profit to be had— only because it seems a fair thing to do.

It must be remembered that those we have discussed are all North American bats. Our bats are basically simple and serve as a very good "starter course" because of that fact. They are, somewhat monotonously, all insect eaters. You will see, as we progress, that bats vary to a degree which seems hardly possible. It is true that they do not swim underwater (although they can swim well enough on top of it when they have to), but they seem to do nearly everything else—from fishing to eating nectar and pollinating flowers. They differ in magnitude from something near hummingbird size to giants with a wingspread of just under six feet, and they vary in physical form from a limpid-eyed ball of fur to a frightful looking apparition which would rival a gargoyle on a buttress of Notre Dame.

One might well wonder why anyone would want to spend a great many years in studying bats. It is true that they have little commercial value, but Fabre studied insects, Pasteur studied germs,

Damien studied death. It is not that one animal or plant, one microorganism or even macrocosm, is more "interesting" or "important" than another. It is simply that things do exist, and that in some deeply subtle way one comes to sense no arithmetic disharmony between a leper, a cosmic explosion, the opening of a flower, and the fluttering of a bat's wing.

5

First
Families

It is all well enough to talk of varied kinds of
bats, to describe their unique adaptations, and
to list the comparisons between divergent types.
The most lucid of descriptive phrasing applied
to bats, however, is useless to us without first
answering: But how did he come to be?

No one knows, really, exactly how the bat came
to be—as no one knows how whales came to be.
Both bats and whales, upon Man's chart of pa-
leontological knowledge, emerge fully matured,
as it were; that is, the most ancient of bats fully
known to be a bat is, plainly and simply, a bat.
It is not a half-bat or part-bat or any other kind
of intermediary bat. So also is the first known
whale still very much of a whale, and only a
whale. It seems odd that the two most peripheral
extremes among mammals should be so strangely
isolated while so many other mammals, such as
horses, for instance, and even Man himself, show
so clearly a marked progression in definable stages.

The ancestry of bats, as is that of every other

41

living thing, is gauged upon the sequence of Geologic Time, that span measurable in the strata of rock. Such time is measured generally not in centuries but in millions of years. The "Time Clock" measuring Geologic Time is divided into three great "Eras" to record the sequence of time: the Paleozoic, Mesozoic, and Cenozoic, words derived from the Greek meaning ancient, middle, and recent. These Eras are in turn divided into "Periods," then the Periods are further divided into "Epochs," much as a clock measures hours, minutes, seconds, and fractions of seconds according to a sequence. Fossils first appeared—as we dig downward—in one of the bottom layers, called the Cambrian Period.

The first *vertebrates* (animals with backbones as compared with invertebrates, animals having none) first appeared in the Ordovician Period, just one rung above the Cambrian in the earliest, the Paleozoic era. These earliest vertebrates were fishlike and simple. Later came the true fishes, the amphibians, reptiles, and birds, and finally the mammals. The dinosaurs, which often first come to our mind when we speak of fossils, are of course reptilian in character, and lived only from the Jurassic Period of the middle era into the Cretaceous Period—a relatively short time. The first mammals appeared during the Jurassic time and were contemporary with the dinosaurs, but the mammals survived while the dinosaurs did not. The first true flying mammals, the bats, did not occur (to our knowledge) until the Eocene

epoch of the Cenozoic or Recent era, when the mammalian order was considerably advanced by perhaps seventy-five million years of evolution. There had been flying animals long before the advent of bats. The pterosaurs, flying reptiles with batlike wings, included the earliest Jurassic form *Rhamphorhynchus*, a small animal about two feet long, as well as *Pteranodon*, a later Cretaceous type, which had a wingspread of about twenty feet. The Jurassic Period also brought forth the first known bird, *Archeopteryx*, a crow-sized animal with feathers but with a somewhat lizardlike head. These contemporaries were endowed with true flight, and, from the reconstructed osteological remains must certainly have been as agile and supple, within certain limitations, as many of our modern flying creatures. But there is little in the morphological characteristics of the true-flight reptilians, adapted through time for their varied ways of life, to link them in any way with the bat. And, to date at least, no "missing link" has arrived on the scene.

We go easily up to the pterodactyls and the first birds—and well we might expect to go on—straight along on a true-flight line to the bats. Not at all. It doesn't take one long, examining the three closely, to throw out entirely any possibility of relationship. Flight itself is not the question. Our search concerns, rather, some clue to a link in the chain of varied adaptations which might have *led* to flight in a mammal, once mammals were established. We try then, the semiflying and nearly-flying (or at least long-jumping) candidates; the flying squirrels, lemurs, and marsupials. All are remarkably adapted for their way of life, but in none of these do we find the one prerequisite which separates all other mammals from the bats:

the singular ability to go progressively *upward*.
The accepted hypothesis and one which seems
sound enough on the face of it—is that the probable ancestor of the bat was a shrewlike animal.
You could hardly be blamed for not knowing
what a shrew is (and Shakespeare will certainly
give you little help). A shrew, tamed or otherwise, is an insectivorous mammal, mouselike in
size but tigerlike in disposition; its teeth are sharp,
generally small, and rather numerous; its nose,
as a rule, is rather longer than you would expect
in a mouse. It is because of the similarity of the
teeth that the shrew—rather, "shrewlike animal"
—is considered by many to be a progenitor of
the bat. From that point on, fancy takes over.
Some authors indulge in long and imaginative
passages about how this slim precursor tired of
terrestrial life and, having taken to the trees, began jumping further and further from limb to
limb, until it "evolved" into a "flying shrew,"
more or less. Other writers simply state flatly
that, as far as they are concerned, it was shrewlike, and that is that. I personally hold with the
latter.

The earliest bats known are from the middle
Eocene epoch, or, roughly, about fifty-five million years old. (The pterodactyls and the first
birds were much older—from the Jurassic Period
—possibly of a time nearing 130 million years
ago.) These first bats in no way resembled anything shrewlike. They were in life bats, and their
fossil bones remain today those of bats, purely
and simply. There are no known intermediate
steps in bat evolution; he was fully formed when
we found him. Considering the time involved, and
in view of the appearance and development of
other mammals, it would seem that the bat is

Shrew

either one of the most ancient of mammals or (more probably) that it passed through a period of very rapid evolution prior to man's discovery of its presence.

The most primordial of bats, actually just a fragment of a lower jaw, was described in 1917 by Dr. W. D. Matthew. This was probably the "first bat," and antedates those Middle Eocene specimens first mentioned, having been found in the older Eocene near Ignacio, Colorado. Matthew gave it the most satisfying name of *Zanyctheris*, meaning "very much of a bat." However, the name now seems oddly inappropriate, for this fragment has become the cause of considerable controversy under the scrutiny of later authorities. Its status is so controversial, in fact—its being considered quite as likely to have been a terrestrial insectivore as a bat—that it is as well passed over.

It is remarkable, considering their delicacy, that many of the most ancient of known bats have come down to us in a very good state of preservation. The greater number come from the Middle Eocene near Darmstadt, Germany. Of thirty-eight specimens, some, preserved nearly in their entirety in slate, were measurable and in such condition as to allow comparison with modern genera. The only really discernible difference between the fossil and modern bats lies in a slight variation in the dental structure and in the spinal column. Some of these fossils strongly resemble specific present-day genera, but certain primitive characteristics are indicated, for instance, no regression in numbers of teeth, a comparative reduction in the length of the forearm as compared to the bone of the upper arm (Allen). In the matter of teeth it was observed that in some of the fossil genera they seemed more like those of insectivores and to lack some of the refinements of modern genera, e.g., having the "milk" or deciduous teeth recurved, an adaptation useful for clinging to the mother's fur. These early bats were given such names as *Palaeochiropteryx* ("early hand-winged") and *Archaeonycteris* ("ancient night flier")—somewhat vague names, really, because in all truth in the disarticulated and sometimes isolated bones themselves there was really little to differentiate the genera in any more radical way.

But hold, now! It is easily enough done—too easily done—to simply sit back like a gaping fish and swallow anything we are fed. Among scientists there is always talk of comparisons and theories and hypotheses and Heaven-only-knows-what of jargon and (to us) gibberish. Might we not only question the validity of such findings, but, as well, scan the process by which such conclusions are drawn?

Of the first—the validity—you and I, as lay-men, must simply rely upon the moral integrity of scientists whose work it is to decipher the puzzles of the past. I can assure you, from my experience among them, that we are in trustworthy hands—although unthinking acceptance of scientific (or any other) dogma is hardly a credit to one's intellectual capacity.

The second question, however, is one I personally chose to challenge; that is, talk of comparisons themselves seemed not enough—there must, I knew, be a *system* of comparisons. The system which I found, that which regulates and brings order out of chaos, in the matter of comparisons is called *taxonomy*. I do dislike a perpetual bringing up of Greek, as though I were proficient to an extreme, and able at a moment's consideration to spew forth derivatives after the fashion of balls from a Roman candle. I can tell you I do not. I painfully look them up one after another, to confirm and reconfirm that which I mean to impart.

Taxonomy is from the Greek τάχις "arrangement," and νόμος "law," or "arrangement according to law." But how did taxonomy get its start? Who first said, "See here, we must be sensible about this sort of thing?" The first taxonomist, or at least the first recorded taxonomist, was Aristotle. Aristotle is someone we all know, and with historic significance it was indeed Aristotle who first said (publicly and for the record, at least) that "we must have a sensible rule—a definite set of laws—in order to set our reasoning right and in order to assure posterity of our exact meaning in relation to the things of which we speak."

It is not my place to write of the historical significance of Aristotle, nor laboriously to set down his history. I should simply be parroting someone else, and even were I inclined to, you would find me out in short order. This sort of information any schoolboy, having the will to do so, can find in an encyclopedia. It is enough that we can regard Aristotle as having been the Prime Mover of it all. I have been convinced of this. I consider it to be historically proved. What I do wish to recount is the sequence of successive contributors since Aristotle in order that you will see that they (those who work with and deal, by way of direction, in these things) have a sound and syllogistic background upon which to base their hypotheses.

The Aristotelian view of animal classification was relatively simple: each different animal was named one by one with its own name, "man," "dog," "horse," "bird," "fish," "serpent," but not in a way which might show interrelationship. The *Cetacea*, whales, were given a separate classification apart from the fishes because of their blowhole and lungs instead of gills. Mammals were truly enough called "hairy, viviparous quadrupeds."

Aristotle's classification remained unaltered for nearly two thousand years. It comprised only the rudimentary verities at best and was filled with gaping errors. But it did last, for the very good reason that no one bothered to do anything else.

Even in 1558 when Conrad Gesner published his *Historia Animalium* at Zurich, he used Aristotle's classification. Wotton published his *Differentiis Animalium* in Paris during the same period, and he, too, used much the same sort of system.

The first real progress was not made until John Ray, son of a blacksmith but later a learned priest and tutor, published in 1693 the *Synopsis Meth-*

odica. This was a great advance over the Aristotelian theories. The simple names were marshaled under generic groupings based upon simple external characteristics, such as hoofs, horns, teeth, and claws. Such terms were used as "Solidiped" for horses, donkeys, and zebras, "Quadrusulate" for the four-toed rhinoceros, and "Dicholate" for cloven-hoofed animals. The Dicholate animals were further divided into those with permanent horns and those, such as deer, with horns which were shed and grown annually. Carnivores were separated into "large, with long muzzles," the dogs; and "large, with short muzzles," the cats. Smaller carnivores such as the weasel were called "small, with long body and short legs." Outside all "known" bounds of classification were certain animals neither Ray nor anyone else would venture to systematize, such as the hedgehogs, armadillos, shrews, and moles, and, of course, the bat. Aristotle well knew about bats. He called it "the bat," but would go no further. Ray went so far as to place these odd residual animals into a separate classification known only as "Anomala," or, "differing from the common rule."

Modern taxonomy and nomenclature began with Linnaeus, in 1758, in his *Systema Naturae.* The point of real departure was his switch in emphasis from the hoofs and horns to the teeth, the system to which, basically, we still adhere. Linnaeus also brought attention to the fact that the hairy quadrupeds were not only live-bearing but suckled from mammae; that is, we—all of us— were "mammals."

Linnaeus was a great step forward. He not only counted the teeth but made note of their position and function. His classification separated the primates from the quadrupeds, and through differ-

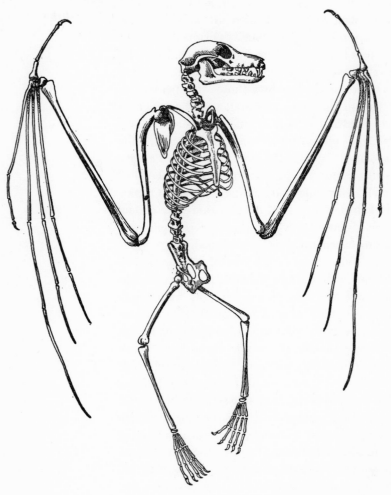

Skeletal structure
(*Pteropus*, a Giant
Fruit bat,
lacking tail)

ences in the teeth as well as in general form, the rodents, horses, and ungulates were separated from other animals. The division *Ferae* contained the carnivores and a good portion of Ray's *Anomala*, including the bat. But still there appeared to be a certain random switching around of things for convenience' sake, presumably, for certain of Ray's arrangements seemed more sound.

The Linnaean hypothesis went through ten revisions. In the tenth edition the class *Mammalia* is first named, so it is actually from this revision that we can date our modern inception. In this edition also, however, Linnaeus made a howling reversal by placing the bat not among the "odd" animals, nor among the four-footed *Ferae*, but in the same category as *Man!* It is supposed that he was led astray by the location of the mammae, which, in many genera, resemble a woman's breasts.

After Linnaeus came Cuvier and Lamarck, contemporaries in late eighteenth- and early nineteenth-century France. The men were highly contrasting figures, competitive colleagues at the Musée Nationale d'Histoire Naturelle. Cuvier was as impatient and schemingly ambitious as Lamarck was gentle and unassuming. The two men worked along similar lines, the purpose of which was to improve and clarify the classification of Linnaeus. Cuvier, basically a comparative anatomist, was to emerge as the father of modern paleontology, while Lamarck, even long after his death, was to be involved in the intense arguments concerning evolution. In their own time, however, the combined effect was to bring still more order to some of the chaotic fringes of the *Systema Naturae*.

Dr. A. Tindall Hopwood of the British Museum (N.H.), one of the leading authorities on historical as well as applied taxonomy, has said, "Cuvier and Lamarck were very nearly the last of the system-makers in zoology; after them there was an ever-growing trend toward the eclecticism of the present day." I think there can be no doubt of it. Darwin, in 1859, had apparently, according to Hopwood, "very little effect on the principles of taxonomy." Darwin did, of course, initiate sweeping reforms in the concepts of natural selection and, perhaps, was responsible for changing the course of history. *Since* Darwin, as Hopwood suggests, the principal trend has not been toward developing new doctrines but toward choosing from different existing sources in order to further clarification—basically from sources laid down by Cuvier and Lamarck. The bat, last seen perched ridiculously next to Man, was given his proper place as a separate entity within the Order of Mammals before even the entrance of Darwin upon the scene, and so he remains today. Modern taxonomists are enriching their inheritance by widening and correlating the knowledge left to them and by the examination of new facets opened to them through advanced technology. But the Latin root of fossil is still *fossus*, meaning "dug up," and unless the earth yields up the key, the mystery of the bat may never be answered in full, to taxonomists or anyone else.

Fossil bats have come from both the Old World and the New, and from strata of varying levels and ages. It can be logically surmised that most of the fossil bats found are those of cave-dwelling species. The reason behind this thinking is that where bats congregate in numbers over long periods of time, there is a far greater chance for

individuals to fall, die, and be covered before they disintegrate by the soft silt which later solidifies and preserves skeletal form. It is not impossible, however, that tree bats or other non-cave-dwelling bats could also have been fossilized and may num- ber among the known collections.

Most of the bats found in fossil form seem to be of the smaller, insect-eating variety, and most commonly represent living bats of the more simple or primitive types. A larger form was found, however, in the fossil beds of Oligocene age near Monteviale, Italy. This bat closely resembled our modern fruit bat except that its teeth seem to be intermediate in form, still retaining certain characteristics of the insectivorous families, and so could possibly be a connecting link between the two—now widely divergent—types.

The bat, then, whether he be of an extinct or living type, or something unknowably in between, remains an enigma. It might be well to offer a brief "Primer on the Bat" before going on to anything more complex. And so:

THE BAT: A PRIMER

A. What he is:

1. His origin is presumed to be from a small shrewlike mammal (roughly the size of a mouse but with very different and more primitive teeth). He somehow evolved to absolute flight, possibly as a further step from an arboreal leap such as the gliding of "flying" squirrels. His skeletal structure is much the same as in other mammals except for extreme modification in length and a less massive total weight of bone as a further concession to actual flight.

2. His exterior is entirely mammalian: there is always hair in greater or lesser quantity; there are external genital organs; and there are mammae, the number of which vary. The senses are often elaborately overdeveloped or underdeveloped, one not infrequently in radical subjugation to another; but there are no "extra" attributes or functions. The young are born alive and are given parental care.

3. Color in bats closely follows the limits of terrestrial mammals; there is never the brilliance of birds, but bright hues are not uncommon and sharply contrasting patterns are not infrequent.

B. *What he does:*
1. The bat's primary function is to serve as the mammalian contribution to "police" the realm of the air much as the cetaceans are adapted to live in and contribute toward keeping a balance of nature within the limits of the sea. Of course all orders of animals and plants contribute their share toward this delicately balanced harmony. Each class has its representatives in each major element of land, sea, and air. The bat is to the dog as the robin is to the ostrich.

2. Basic food habits are nearly as diverse as those of terrestrial mammals. There are no ungulate or "grazing" types of bats, nor are there polar species. There are, however, carnivorous, insectivorous, and frugivorous bats, and even flower-eaters, the last of which might well parallel herbivorous land animals such as rabbits.

Facing page:
Anatomy of the bat

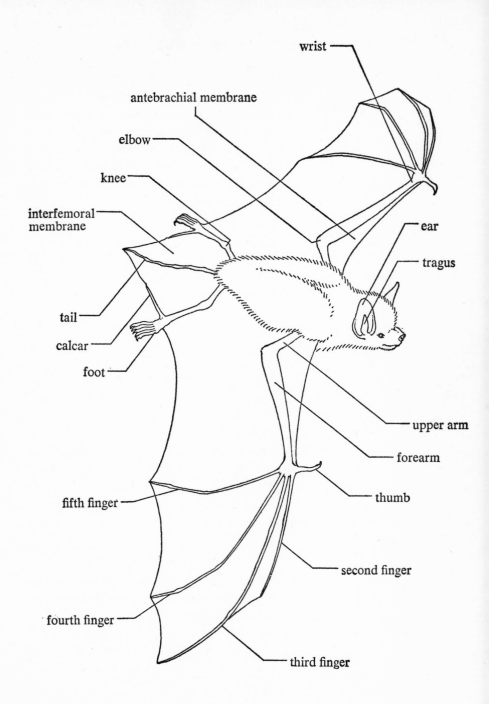

wrist

antebrachial membrane

elbow

knee

interfemoral
membrane

ear

tragus

tail

calcar

foot

upper arm

forearm

fifth finger

thumb

second finger

fourth finger

third finger

3. The bat does not make a "nest" in the ordinary sense, although certain genera do alter tropical leaves to shelter themselves more adequately. As a rule the bat lives either in the shelter of caves or similar terrestrial recesses, or in the shelter of the leaves, branches, or hollows of trees. The houses of man, a very recent innovation in the span of Time, are used only as alternative shelters.

6

The Social Register

In the city of New York there is a black book
bearing two thin trilinear red lines on its cover
(these by way of decoration). Within this book
are names, addresses, clubs, schools . . . there are
sons' names, daughters' names, and a very lovely
scattering of pertinent information. This book
tells one who one is, where one must live, what
to join, and whom to marry. It tells one how to
succeed in business and how to get to Heaven—
or at least how to get to Heaven in Good Taste.

You and I—and some millions of others—may
or may not be in this particular book. But we are
in other books. One might think that Literature,
Science, Religion, even encyclopedic knowledge
or any grand thing toward which men might as-
pire—that these or one of many others might lead
the world in sheer bulk of output. Surely they do
not. What does lead the world in bulk is the off-
spring (or progenitors) or at any rate the associ-
ates of the black book; for better or for worse it is
the ROSTER. *Everyone*—barring perhaps only

some hyperborean Eskimo or Patagonian hermit
—virtually everyone is *listed*. If not on the Queen's
Honours List or in the Almanach de Gotha,
then in the Loyal Order of the Moose . . . if not
the United Asparagus Growers Union, it is the
Knights of Pythias or the Middletown Township
Rescue Squad. If one abhors all societies, major
and minor, there is always the telephone book. If
your retirement forbids you even the phone, the
church gets at you . . . and even beyond God there
lies the tax collector (*he* knows where you are!).
And so, as surely as we are marked in life, some
calligraphic fool follows us into the ground with
an epitaph. We are marked as surely as we live,
and by someone, accurately or inaccurately, we
are categorically placed.

The easiest of us to recognize are those of us
in uniforms: policemen, mail carriers, ice-cream
vendors, generals of armies, doormen, and priests
—all are, or should be, exactly what their exterior badge informs us they are. Nonuniformed
people are harder, though not impossible, to recognize: a plumber carries plumber's tools and,
presumably, plumbs (if you can catch him at it);
a banker dresses, talks, and lives such a gloriously
staid and conservative life that we are assured his
wife, his children, his self-control, and *our money*
are all in hands so steady, so safe, so firmly capable, that even when he jumps out of a window
this impression of good, gray soundness is so in-
grained we "cannot believe it possible"; the doctor
carries a black bag and simply reeks with com-
petence; the painter has flecks of paint on his
shoes . . . and it goes on.

My point is this: as we are superficially marked,
numbered, and catalogued, so also, but more profoundly, is every living thing "listed." I do not

mean to imply that there is a petroglyphic record-
ing incised by some Unseen Recorder: I do mean
that any living thing is most certainly in relation
to another and can be recognized. The squirrel
belongs in trees as properly as leaves, the otter is
a submarine torpedo that outswims fishes, and the
cat is a nearly perfect engine of destruction. There
is an order and harmony, sphere within sphere,
the magnitude and dimension of which is staggering. A telephone book is a well-spring of what
bounds in poetry!

Bats, as living things, are divided and subdi-
vided as are we, not only by what they are, but
by what they do. It is pleasant and secure to be
able to recognize a soldier because of his uniform,
but it is warmly gratifying, not without the spice
of adventure, to discern the poet under the façade
of a stockbroker or the gardener behind the
bruised countenance of a prize fighter. People—
and animals—are genuinely what they are, no
matter what, but they are not always that which
they appear to be.

The bat whom we know—the personal bat, the
bat of our childhood and of our lamplight, *our*
bat—is only one of many kinds. How are we to
divide them? The scientist has borrowed from the
child: the large ones are called *Megachiroptera*
and the smaller *Microchiroptera*—quite literally,
"large" and "small." But as with most things
there is the eternal question as to what is "large"
and what is "small"—and, to make it worse, there
are small "*Mega-*" and quite large "*Microchiroptera.*" There is one irrefutable point however: the
Megachiroptera are found only in the Old World
and are characterized by the total absence of a
tragus—that peculiar "guard lobe" on the ear.
They also have an extra "claw" on the first digit.

Although the *Megachiroptera* are often called "fruit bats," this is not a good term, for there are fruit-eating bats among the *Microchiroptera*.

MEGACHIROPTERA

As to what, exactly, is "large" and "small," we must rely on comparisons. The *Megachiroptera* are not gargantuan by some standards, but as bats, or rather, as we know bats, many of them are very large indeed. The largest is just under six feet in wingspread. These bats are generally fruit-eaters, and, in spite of their size, are quite harmless to all mankind except orchard growers. Where they are found in abundance, they can be a serious pest, but not to the extent of being calamitous. It is these bats which, as has been said, are a food staple in the parts of the world where they occur. They are relatively heavy, two to three pounds, and even the smaller species of the group are solidly built and "firm of flesh." In general, these bats are a rather handsome lot, comparatively, that is; their faces are often so doglike one is tempted to compare them with canine breeds; their fur, though less dense and fine than in the smaller bats, is often strikingly contrasted and quite rich in color; their limbs are well muscled and supple and their eyes are large, bright, and possessed often of that odd look animals sometimes have which gives the impression of genuine intelligence.

The various genera represented in the *Megachiroptera* feed almost exclusively on fruit, flowers, pollen, or nectar. Their appetites are voracious and their taste, within the realm of fruit or their specific specialty, is limitless. Each genus seems to have some predilection toward at least one or another of delicacies, however, and some are most tenacious in the pursuit of their favorite food.

The great fruit bats are social creatures, establishing themselves in "camps" of sometimes countless thousands. These camps—so called— are simply "hanging areas" in trees where often the weight of numbers causes the branches to bend nearly to the ground. If these areas are occupied for very long periods, the accumulation of droppings of excrement has been known to denude nearly all the underfoliage, so great are the masses. Since these bats are quarrelsome as well as gregarious, the din of their colony can often be heard over a mile away. The camps are seldom permanent, for the bats are nomadic and migrate to other feeding grounds as sources of food diminish.

The breeding season of these bats, in spite of the more or less constant tropical temperature, seems to be as strictly regulated as it is with animals living under seasonal conditions. It has been observed that the gestation period is generally about six months in the larger species, and that the young, in nearly all cases, seem to be born in August or September.

I have spoken of "uniforms" and of "work." This has not been an attempt to anthropomor-

Pteropus,
the Flying Fox

phize or to reduce to puerile terms. I use this analogy in order more easily to separate one family or genus from another, not merely as a parallel by way of convenience, but because the separations are as genuine among the bats as they are in human society. We say that a man is a "policeman," "farmer," or "fisherman," not with any sense of embellishment, but because it is true. The separations in the large bats are not as spectacular or varied as among the *Microchiroptera;* in most cases they are one type or another of "farmer" or "fruiterer," though of course their position is always that of consumer and seldom producer (except by way of distributing seeds, which service they do render).

The family name of the larger fruit bats is *Pteropodidae,* and the largest of these are generally called *Pteropus.* These are the bats commonly called "flying foxes." Their "uniforms" vary greatly between species, but one indicative mark is the presence of a "mantle" of brighter fur including or bordering the head and generally ending low on the shoulders at a line of demarcation of darker fur. These giants of their kind are all from the Australasian region. They are without a tail, have the most canine-appearing of heads, and in some species their wings stretch to well over five feet—nearly to six.

Rousettus,
the Dog-faced bat

Another of the large bats—with a wingspread of over three feet—is *Hypsignathus* of Africa, the so-called "Hammer-headed" or "Horse-faced" bat. He has a grotesque, greatly swollen muzzle, and numerous wartlike appendages on the lips. This bat has also a much enlarged larynx, which acts as a sounding board to boom a very loud *"pwok,"* dwarfing the other sounds of jungle night. His diet consists mostly of fruit juices.

Still others include the Australian *Dobsonia*, a specialized fruit bat with the lower part of the back naked and the wings attached to the body only at the spinal juncture, giving somewhat of a "parachute" effect; the smaller East Indian *Cynopterus*, one of the few bats to make a "house" for itself by gnawing away the seed clusters of palms; and widely spread *Rousettus*. Altogether there are over thirty genera of *Pteropodidae*.

Among the smaller (but still under the classification of *Mega-*) fruit bats are the Oriental flower-eating *Eonycteris*; the African *Micropteropus*, a pigmy among fruit bats, measuring only 2.75 inches in length and with a mere eleven-inch wingspread. Among the most delicate and finely wrought of all the *Megachiroptera* is the nectar-eating *Syconycteris*, a tiny, long-nosed, feather-tongued, ball of fur from Australia. We caught them high in the New Guinea mountains in Japanese mist nets of finest silk. They look for all the world like diminutive teddy bears.

Dobsonia,
the Spinal-winged
Flying Fox

The smaller fruit bats, as you can see, range in size from near-giant to quite small—smaller, as we have said, than many of those listed under *Microchiroptera*. These are included among the *Megachiroptera*, however, because they are simply

Hypsignathus,
Horse-faced Fruit bat

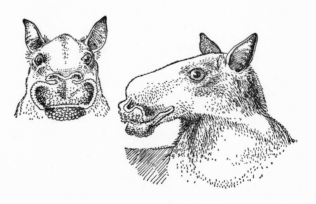

smaller editions, so to speak, of the larger fruit bats and lack the tragus.

But before we go on to our *Micro-* bats, we should mention among the more curious of the *Megachiroptera, Nyctimene*—named after the Greek goddess of night. More commonly called the Tube-nosed bat, its nostrils are periscopic in character, turning abruptly upward; a theoretical explanation gives credit to evolution's having solved the problem of continually having one's nose in one's soup—as likely an explanation as any since mushy fruit could conceivably be a problem. The animal is further adorned with a wide dorsal stripe, a massive but somehow appealing "square-jawed" look, and the most ridiculous paint-spattered pattern of yellow and white on its wings, ears, and stumpy tail. And to top it off, *Nyctimene* often has a saffron-yellow muzzle and penis.

A much smaller *Nyctimene*, included among the smaller fruit bats, is the more delicate *Paranyctimene*, a tube-nosed bat with refinements in both coloration and morphology.

The effect upon mankind by these flying vegetarians is often exaggerated. They do indeed cause certain damage to fruit trees, often extensive damage. But they also spread seeds and so replenish the supply of trees, and they serve as food to thousands of protein-starved people.

MICROCHIROPTERA

There is an American paint company which boasts a slogan occasionally flashed from great electric signs. In fiery letters we are told that this paint "covers the earth"—and a neon globe is every few seconds doused with a flood of red which does just that.

I feel, as I have before me a closely-written list of the *Microchiroptera*, that they not only cover, but like that paint sign, they literally flood the earth. I hesitate about just where to begin, for there would seem to be simply too many; they are legion—and each seems more weird than the last. There are such wild and fantastic shapes, sizes, and adaptations (one is almost tempted to call them "deformities") that they present, as a collage, a most frightening aspect.

The purposes served by the *Microchiroptera* vary greatly. The greatest number are insect-eaters but there are fish-eating, fruit-eating, bird-eating, blood-drinking, and even cannibal bats, all of them listed under the *Microchiroptera*.

Their "uniforms" are as varicolored as their appetites are universal, ranging from bright hues of reds and yellows to dull umbers, spotted white or black, even to pure white. And their "equipment" covers every conceivable sort of variation from sloe-eyed innocence to the fantastic.

The extremes of specialization found in these bats are highly intricate. One is certainly given to wonder "why" all of this should be. Some variations are clearly evident as to purpose, but in utmost frankness, it must be said there is much we do not know concerning the exact reasons for many of these extraordinary adaptations. There are those who hold that evolutionary change is betimes slipshod, perhaps, in forming certain sports or deviations which differ from what could be called a more "normal" physiognomy. It is not

my business to challenge such theories, but it would seem, in the matter of certain startling adaptive conformations, that rather than Creation having been so unarithmetic, and even downright sloppy, perhaps man has not yet learned all the answers.

As we have learned, nearly all of our own American varieties are of the *Vespertilionidae*, or Simple-nosed bats. I do believe that ours are a rather solid, staid, and pretty much down-to-earth sort. No nonsense about them generally; just good, sound bats, one would say. There is an occasional long ear or lumpy nose, but there are few to frighten one out of a year's growth.

Miniopterus,
the Bent-winged bat

But the *Vespertilionidae* vary to considerable degree within their own group, ranging from the most simply contrived *Myotis* (our common Little Brown bat) to the giant-eared *Plecotus*. They are not restricted to the tropics or either hemisphere but are world-wide in distribution, being found from the most equatorial latitudes to the very fringes of the true Arctic. They are specialized in that they are indeed bats, but beyond that they are not of consummate interest. If any qualify as such, the *Vespertilionidae* would stand first as what might be called "typical" bats; that is, they have "wings," but "wings" not too large nor too oddly proportioned; they have fur, but fur neither too scant nor too long; their eyes are adequate but nothing more; their teeth are quite good for chewing insects and their noses are quite as unimaginative as our own, being simply noses, quite plain and unobtrusive.

Kerivoula,
Painted bat

The *Vespertilionidae* also vary greatly in relative abundance within their family. The ubiquitous *Myotis*, for instance, is represented by over 80 species; *Eptesicus* by 45, and *Pipistrellus* by

40, while many others are represented by only the single (or at best by few) species.

The large family of Simple-nosed bats is divided into six major groups, scientifically termed *subfamilies* (you will notice how the family plural suffix *-idae* changes to *-inae* in order to designate subfamily).

The *Vespertilioninae* or Typical Simple-nosed bats, are world-wide in distribution, ranging from the northernmost limits at which bats are to be found into the deepest tropics. They vary from small to medium in size, are all insect-eaters, and, whether in the heart of Africa or in the wilds of New Guinea, behave exactly as do bats here at home. There are over 250 species represented by 34 genera in this subfamily alone.

The *Miniopterinae*, or Bent-winged bats, unlike the deluge in numbers we have just left, are limited to a single genus. They are also limited to the tropics and subtropics of the Old World and their principal departure from the norm is in the wing tips, the third finger of which is lengthened and arranged so as to fold under while at rest. The head is also very highly "domed."

The Tube-nosed insectivorous bats, *Murininae*, are divided into three genera and are entirely Asian in distribution. The "tube-noses" are much more simplified than in *Nyctimene* of the *Mega*-group.

The *Kerivoulinae*, the Painted bats, are very delicate and pretty little animals. They have very large, funnel-shaped ears and a long, pointed tragus. The fur is bright and long and is reddish-yellow in color. There are two genera, *Kerivoula* and *Phoniscus*, ranging from Africa into south Asia and New Guinea.

The *Nyctophilinae*, or Big-eared bats, consist

Hipposideros diadema, the largest Horseshow bat

of three genera, one in the New World and two in the Old. *Antrozous* is found in the western United States and ranges to central Mexico. *Nyctophilus* and *Pharotis* are found chiefly in Australia, New Guinea, and some South Pacific islands. They are more specialized *Vespertilionidae* in which small nose-leaves are developed. The ears are very large and are joined at the base.

Tomopeatinae is but a single genus, *Tomopeas*, and is restricted to Peru. It is remarkable in that it seems to combine the characteristics of the *Vespertilionidae* with those of the *Molossidae* or Free-tail bats. It has the long tail and full membrane of the former, but the ear structure and a peculiar fusion of neck vertebrae of the latter. It is thought to be a possible ancestral type, partially bridging the gap between the two families.

These six subfamilies, then, the Simple-nosed bats, seemingly intricate enough, are now to be left behind. There is no such thing, really, as a "typical" bat, but the *Vespertilionidae*, I think you will agree before we finish, are as "simple" as bats come.

Our departure from the "normal" becomes most rapid. The so-called "Horseshoe" bats, consisting of two families, the *Rhinolophidae* and *Hipposideridae*, are Old World species. In flight, general habits, and in procurement of food they are much the same as the Simple-nosed bats. But even the most casual examination from closer up will reveal an astonishing departure from anything which might be referred to as "simple." Their noses seem to have an unending variety of fleshy appendages: flattened horsehoe-shaped ovals, with "whorls," "polyps," "leaves," and "spears" —all most distinct individually but having enormous variance between species.

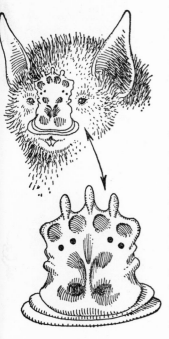

Enlarged nose-leaf of *Aselliscus*, a rare bat from New Guinea

In earlier years *Hipposideros* was considered to be merely a kind of *Rhinolophus*. The genus *Rhinolophus* was first used by Lacépède in 1799; *Hipposideros*, coming later, by the rules of taxonomic priority, was bound to follow in a subordinate role if the two remained under the same name. They are closely linked, but certainly would seem to warrant distinct division. *Rhinolophus*, as wild-looking a chap as ever haunted a cave, has among other notable characteristics one particular oddity in obvious distinction from Hipposiderine bats: a fleshy "spear" of singular appearance crowning the leafy nose. Also, *Rhinolophus* remains alone in his category. The *Hipposideridae*, as a family, contain not only the numerous species under the genus *Hipposideros* but also the genera *Anthops, Aselliscus, Rhinonycteris, Trianeops*, and others; all of which differ in many ways from either main form but are allied to *Hipposideros* rather than to *Rhinolophus* chiefly because of a reduction of pedal phalanges and by the absence of a third premolar.

The account given above, all of which is true, will serve one purpose at least. If you have been so brave as to wade waist-deep through it, it will give an indication of the complexity of these bats, not only in form and numbers, but in their scientific division, which is still a subject of active controversy.

These bats themselves—that is, taken away from the web of scientific nomenclature—are a sociable and friendly lot. They range from small to moderate in size and are of varied colors, though most run to reds and browns. They are mainly cave-dwellers and with little objection share their homes with other kinds of bats.

Since we seem to be perhaps inordinately in-

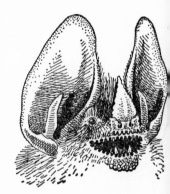

Trachops,
a Tropical American
Fringe-lipped bat

Carollia,
the Short-tailed
Fruit bat of
Tropical America

Mormoops,
the Leaf-chinned bat

Phyllonycteris,
of Tropical America

volved with noses it might be well to rid ourselves of them, as it were, with the proscribed and not unbatlike "one swoop." What exactly, does "Leaf-nose" mean?

All "common names" are in some way misleading. We have spoken of Simple-nosed, Horseshoe-nosed, and now Leaf-nosed bats. The terms mean very little, really, except as "tags" or vague labels of identity, much as we might employ abbreviated names such as "Bob," "Dick," and "Ned." These nicknames tell us nothing except that Dick is not Ned or someone else. There may be a half-dozen Dicks or a score of Neds. We really get nowhere until we hear the surname, clearly and distinctly. But with our charges, the bats, included under given families, even their "surnames" will do us little good unless each is carefully translated from the Latin and interrelated with others of similar nature. Even then there is the danger of simply too many five- and six-syllable words to coordinate one with the other. "Leaf-nosed" may not mean much, but perhaps it is better at first than a rapid-fire cacophony of such names as *Phyllostomatidae*, *Chalionycterinae*, and *Dolichophyllum*. We must certainly name things properly, and we shall do so, but as an introductory appellation "Leaf-nosed" will do.

The Leaf-nosed bats—designated *Phyllostomatidae* by the taxonomist—are all bats of the New World. Nearly all are tropical or near-tropical species. Their range, then, since the New World is very narrow compared with the Old, is that strip of land and adjacent islands reaching from the extreme southern portions of the United States, crossing the narrowed Panamanian isthmus, the equator, and continuing southward into South America until the tropics are left behind, at an approximate latitude of 30° south.

Considering that their scope is at least narrowed laterally, the *Phyllostomatidae* certainly are both numerous and varied. Again as in the *Vespertilionidae*, they are principally divisible into seven major subfamilies:

The *Chilionycterinae*, or Leaf-chinned bats, which have *no* nose-leaf and look as though they were some product of an Aesopian turn-about made to wear their ornamentation upside down; the *Phyllostomatinae*, Typical Leaf-nosed bats, Mephistophelian in appearance, carnivorous, and the largest (to thirty-inch wingspread) of American bats; the *Carolliinae*, Tricolored Short-tailed fruit bats, have a short tail, a spear-nose, and warted lower lip, and, in addition, a distressing habit of defecating when forced to make abrupt turns, the result being that houses and people are not infrequently spattered with feces (Goodwin and Greenhall); the *Sturnirinae* or Epaulet fruit bats have no external tail and glandular "shoulder patches" of stiff hairs; the *Glossophaginae* or Nectar-feeding bats resemble those of the Old World except for the presence of a tragus and a pronounced spear-nose; the *Phyllonycterinae*, another group of nectar-feeding bats, in which the nose-leaf is even more refined; and (finally) the *Stenoderminae* or Broad-faced fruit bats, all of which have very broad heads. Among the last-mentioned is a genus named *Centurio*, which is among the most unusual of all bats: he boasts nothing that resembles a nose-leaf, but has a gargoyle face formed entirely of fleshy folds while the weird lips are covered with small papillae which seem to act as food strainers. Another of the genera, *Uroderma*, is among the few bats which make a shelter or "house," in this case by biting the fanned-

Artibeus,
a Tropical American
fruit bat

Centurio,
the Wrinkle-faced bat
of Tropical America

out surface of a Carat palm leaf, causing the frond to bend at an angle to form a protective haven.

These six subfamilies, as we have mentioned, include all of the genera named under the Leaf-nosed bats. In a way this family would seem to be a South American version of many types of bats found in the Old World. Certainly the Old and New World families differ widely, but they are all bats and fill the same niches in their respective regions. The only logical explanation seems to be that the Prime Progenitor Bat was indeed "very much of a bat" (as Matthew would have it) and some time after he had traveled from the place of his conception—for he must surely have initially come from one region and not simply "popped out" at various places simultaneously— he saw his progeny evolve into quite distinct geographical groups. But why are some groups distinctly New or Old World and others world-wide in distribution? Have certain groups which thrive in one world died out entirely in the other? Why should some be isolated, such as the American *Phyllostomatidae*, while others, such as the *Emballonuridae*, a world-wide family not at all isolated, be seen to commingle with the "isolated" *Phyllostomatidae*? If one could "fly in" could not the other have "flown out"? These, and many other questions, are tantalizing subjects for conjecture.

Lonchorhina,
Tome's Leaf-nosed bat

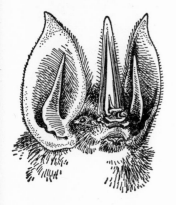

And again we must remark on the inconsistencies found in the common names. There are other bats which upon occasion will catch and eat fish; *Pizonyx*, a Mexican Vespertilionid, is one, and the Asian *Myotis rickettia* is suspected of having a fish diet. But certainly the bats called *Noctilionidae* are well worthy of the name "fish-eating," for they are just that. This family pos-

Choeroniscus,
the Trinidadian
Long-nosed bat

sesses very long limbs, large feet, and strong, sharp claws to serve as fishhooks. They are medium to large in size, have narrow, sharp-pointed ears and short, orange-brown, close fur with a narrow white dorsal stripe. *Noctilio*, one of two genera, often lives in sea caves and frequently flies during the late afternoon and early morning in company with pelicans and other fish-eating birds. This bat catches small fish by skimming over the surface of the water, his long legs and feet hanging down to snatch his prey from the waves. The fish are sometimes eaten in flight (the chewing sound is often audible) or carried in large cheek pouches back to the roost and eaten there (Goodwin). Roosting sites always smell strongly of fish and often the tree or cavern is plastered with tiny, sparkling fish scales which brilliantly reflect the morning sunlight. *Noctilio* is American, ranging from Cuba and Mexico to northern Argentina. The family contains only two species, with, oddly enough, distinct habits and tastes: *Noctilio leporinus* is the fisherman, while *Noctilio albiventer* is insectivorous.

Taphozous australus, a Sheath-tailed Tomb bat from Australia

Hollow-faced bats, the *Nycteridae*, are represented by a single genus *Nycteris*. The fact that these bats range from Africa to the East Indies, and are solely forest bats, has prompted some inquirers to speculate that a continuous forest once extended from the Congo to the Malay region. They are rightly called "Hollow-faced" for the interorbital part of the skull is deeply dished out, forming less a cleft than a wide pit; this pit is clearly evident beneath the fur on the face and forehead. *Nycteris* is an insect-eater and lives mainly in hollow trees.

Emballonura, Sheath-tailed bat

The Sheath-tailed bats, *Emballonuridae*, are a curious family and certain of them are among the

smallest of bats. They are divided into two sub-families, the *Emballonurinae*, or Sac-winged bats, and the *Diclidurinae*, or White bats. All of these have a reflex-wing—a "double jointing" of the terminal ends of the first two fingers. In rest these digital tips double back to make a much shorter-seeming wing. These bats also have a very short tail, which, as the wings are seen to double-fold, retracts into a sheath of skin in the interfemoral membrane. Besides all of this, many have glandular sacs or pockets in their antebrachial membrane (that anterior membrane which stretches from the shoulder to the wrist).

The *Emballonuridae* are world-wide in distribution, each major land mass having its own varieties as well as sharing certain genera. They are not all cave-dwellers but most are at least semicolonial, being found in small groups but seldom in large colonies. *Taphozous*, one of the larger genera, is a dull umber with very short fur; *Emballonura*, one of the smallest Australasian types, is well-furred.

*Nycteris,
the Hollow-
faced bat*

The *Diclidurinae* is represented by three genera, all of which are nearly pure white in color. As might be expected, they are invariably called Ghost bats. Beyond that they are known more accurately as Sac-tailed bats, since they have a glandular sac near the middle of the interfemoral membrane. They are slender, medium-sized bats and have long, silky hair which is truly white, although the hairs very close to the skin may have a grayish base. Even the membranes and limbs are white, though sometimes they have a yellowish tinge. The eyes are large and dark. They appear to be solitary rather than colonial animals, and are insect-eaters.

The family of *Megadermatidae*, or False vam-

pires, are unusual even among these multitudes
we have been going through. These quite large
bats are the "Cannibal bats," preying upon smaller bats, birds, or even small terrestrial animals.
They are strongly built and most impressive if
taken alive; their long, razor-sharp teeth and general atmosphere of power is enough to implant
caution in the most reckless human. There are
four genera, each of which is more or less restricted to a land mass: *Lavia* and *Cardioderma*
are tropical African and east African; *Megaderma*
is Indian and East Indian; and *Macroderma* is
Australian. They are all quite spectacular; the
African *Lavia* is dove-gray with saffron wings and
nose, and *Macroderma* is another Ghost bat with
white wings, great white ears, and a very pale
body. These bats have a large, erect nose-leaf and
very large ears, which are centrally joined for half
their length. They are cave bats. The name *Megaderma*, meaning "large skin," evidently alludes to
the immense nose-leaf and ears. The common
name False vampire is a misnomer most likely
given because it was as wicked a term as could be
conjured up to in any way match the ferocity of
their natures.

There is indeed a true Vampire bat; a bat which
drinks blood. They are remarkable animals but
instead of elaborating upon them here we shall
reserve them for another chapter, for their habits
have been so controversially publicized as to lead
to some confusion.

Then there are the Long-legged and Smoky
bats, *Natalidae* and *Furipteridae*, both tropical
American, which easily go together; each is delicately formed, long-limbed, and long-tailed. They
have simple noses. *Natalus* has an almost thread-
like tail and *Furipterus* has only a rudimentary

thumb. They are insect-feeders and live in caves.

The Disc-winged and Sucker-footed bats, the American *Thyroptera*, and its distant relation in Madagascar, *Myzopoda*, and the Asian *Tylonycteris*, all have one of the most unique adaptations in the mammalian world: fleshy pads which act as sucker discs in the same manner as does the rubber tip on a child's arrow. These discs are remarkable in their adhesive quality, enabling the animals to cling upside down on the smooth surface of a furled banana leaf or on a ceiling.

The Mouse-tailed bat, *Rhinopoma*, the tomb bat of Egypt, still looking down on the Pharaohs as he did when the ancient rulers were laid to rest, and lonely *Mystacina* of New Zealand, perhaps the rarest bat in the world, are each the only member of their respective families. *Mystacina* is thought to be a lone survivor of a once more widely distributed group. The Short-tailed bat, as he is called, has a tail so short as to seem only a stump of something more satisfactory.

Finally, there are the *Molossidae*, the Free-tailed bats, velvet-furred and muscular, with broad and leathery ears which project over the eyes. The thick, naked, and unadorned muzzle is wrinkled and has sparse spoon-shaped hairs. The tail is long and projects well beyond the border of the inter-femoral membrane, giving cause to the common name. Some are also called Mastiff bats, for they have large and forbidding teeth and present a most formidable appearance.

These are our insect-eating "guano" bats which congregate in countless thousands in large caves, found in both the Old and New Worlds.

Are there other bats than these? Most likely there are not. One must remember that only families

The Naked bat, *Cheiromeles*, a Molossid

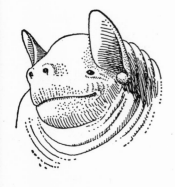

Chaerephon, an African Molossid (after Chapin)

have here been annotated, the genera, numbering over two-hundred, being far too numerous to name in detail. As for the species, they number over two thousand. New bats are still being found, but most are species or subspecies; seldom are they entirely new, as in the case of generic division. There have been reports both in Australia and New Guinea of people who have sworn they have seen a "marsupial bat," but these people never actually appear. I think it can be fairly safely presumed that any marsupial bat has come out of a rum bottle.

Opinions will vary about the animals we have just reviewed. I think all will admit they are curious creatures. If not, at least one must agree that they have been most imaginatively contrived. Definitions of "beauty" and comparisons in "ugliness" are matters which are subject to wide variances, and in every way, really, are quite a personal matter.

Earth's crammed with Heaven
And every common bush afire with God,
But only he who sees takes off his shoes;
The rest sit round it and pluck blackberries.
— ELIZABETH BROWNING

Thyroptera,
a Tropical American
Disc-winged bat
(showing discs)

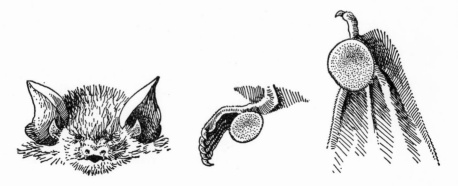

7

Around the World at Twilight

We are going "around the world" more these days. But although the world is no more round nor large than it was to Magellan or to Captain Cook, our modes of conveyance are different. Now we have use of an ancient Chinese device, much older than Magellan, called the rocket. The rockets have succeeded and so has man: he has looked out of their windows and has come back shouting, waving his arms, and brandishing pictures to tell us that the world is round. It is pleasant to know that the world is round; to see these splendid pictures and to listen to man tell us of the awesome arc of night that lies beyond. It is less pleasant to learn that so many centuries of terrestrial Man's achievements and the great and secure land masses we know, as they are seen to pass below, seem as small and insignificant as the infusoria in a drop of water.

But the earth is not so bad, after all. With all the current emphasis on rocketry, it is still large enough to those of us who cannot see it from a distance. A measured mile is still a mile, the "mornings fresh, the evenings smil'd," and one can still feel the soft country dust about one's feet. One thing certainly remains: the old familiar land masses are still much as they were, at least much the same as Man has ever known them. The continents, peninsulas, mountains, and water passages are all the same. The irritable staccato of political subdivision is meaningless to the somnolent land.

We have seen how widely divergent are the kinds of bats which coinhabit our sphere. We have seen, in précis, but with some sort of order, how they live. But, so eager have I been to describe them in detail in terms of their morphological characteristics, I have too hastily, perhaps, passed over a point of great importance: their interrelationships in the light of geographic distribution.

The world is sensibly divided into zones: latitudinal thermal and longitudinal time zones. Animals have no concern with time, geomagnetic pull, and orbital acceleration but they certainly are well aware of being either hot or cold. They are also aware of time, if only of the time to mate and procreate. The zones of greater or lesser warmth are a principal cause in many of our adaptive processes. Where one species cannot adapt itself to a given temperature condition, it can do one of only three things: it can migrate to another clime, it can so adapt itself as to be able to live in the conditions it finds, or, as has often been the case, it can die. Such reasoning, though simple enough in itself, touches upon profundities which are not my business to approach: the complexities of evolution, its historical significance, and its possible genetic functioning at work today. But it is my business to tell the story of the distribution of bats as far as I am able by way of reference to factual data.

To anyone who has ever crossed the equator by sea this zonal difference is vividly apparent. One embarks in New York or London complete with a full array of deciduous woolens, and, nearing the Canal Zone or West Africa, contrives to be as near naked as circumstances will allow. Certainly it can become uncomfortably hot in the "north" with late summer heat, and entirely too cold for Easter in the "south"—but such fickle peregrinations are for the temperate zone only; the arctic and equatorial climes are considerably more dependable. The zones begin at the equator —as the root of the word "zone" indicates, i.e., in both Latin and Greek, a "girdle or belt." The equatorial belt is called the Torrid Zone; the polar extremities, the Frigid Zones, and anything in between them, the Temperate Zones. The lines of demarcation between the Torrid and Temperate Zones are the so-called "Tropics" of Cancer and Capricorn. The Tropics are located exactly 23° 27′ north and south of their respective poles, where the sun reaches its greatest declination, and were named for the two celestial constellations nearest those points at which the tropics touch the ecliptic. All of the area south of Cancer and north of Capricorn is popularly termed "tropics" and remains perpetually warm, as the poles remain cold.

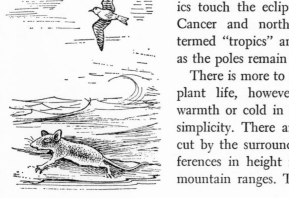

There is more to the distribution of animal and plant life, however, than a liking for either warmth or cold in a latitudinal world of utmost simplicity. There are the thousandfold contours cut by the surrounding seas and the varying differences in height from sea level to the highest mountain ranges. Time, with each revolution of the earth, reveals not only a continually changing topography but a topographic face which is erratic and varied in its apportionment. Scientists have shuffled and rearranged a score or so of appellative "regions," few of which are capable of complete isolation by clearly defined boundaries. All are subject to one type or another of "invasion" from an adjoining region.

How does one type of bird, mammal, plant, or seed travel over vast expanses of water to an entirely different situation in zone and in continental division? Here enters the mythmaker, with his fetching tales of birds carried on hurricane winds and small mammals and seeds borne on flotsam. But here, for once, at least, he must be right. However picturesque the telling, the fact remains that this, that, and the other did naturally occur. By whatever means these transferrals were made it must be recognized that somehow they did occur.

Of course those with wings, back in our mist-shrouded beginnings, must have had a much more rapid transferral than their poor terrestrial cousins. They had the additional advantage of being able, in whatever type of migration they joined, to accept or reject a given climatic or altitudinal region into which they might have blundered. The earth-bound quadruped, blown seaward on a tussock raft, had no such choice when, as did Christian, "he reached the farther shore." Bats, then, along with birds, were among the Household Elite, as it were, being able to pick and choose while the plodding lesser folk (you and I) were allowed to expand only by hit or miss.

There have been varied hypotheses regarding the representation of species in both the Old and New Worlds, ranging from the wildly improbable to some very sound reasoning. Wegener asserted there was a splitting of worlds, one drifting from another. Matthew reasoned that land masses have remained stable except for the fluctuations of tide levels and eruptive forces from within the earth. Such fluctuations might well have caused "land bridges" of a sort on which terrestrial animals could simply have walked across. Allen (1940) adds to Matthew's theory the fact that since cyclic periods of warmer climates are known to have affected the northern latitudes there might have been ample time for certain families of bats to have reached tropical North America without ever having had to cross a frigid belt. Allen, however, also firmly stated that this would scarcely have been accomplished without the chance of considerable loss, accounting, therefore, for such similar but widely separated bats as the Disc-winged of South America and the Sucker-footed bats of Madagascar. Who can tell what extremes of allied types might not have perished in complete anonymity along the way?

The subject of distribution in bats has not been widely theorized by great numbers of people. The few who have considered this problem have given it great thought and exhaustive study. However, as with the original hypotheses concerning evolution, after a certain point is reached there is the inevitable reliance on eclecticism. We have reviewed certain principal names in tracing the pattern of general taxonomic treatment of animals. There were others who gave the bat more attention, notably Lesson (1827, 1852); Bonaparte (1838); Gervais (1855); Gray (1866); Gill (1872); Dobson (1875); Winge (1892); Weber (1904); and finally Miller (1907). There have in-

deed been masterful studies along regional and
even continental lines, and most interesting inquiries into fossil remains, but not since Miller in
1907 has anything new been offered as to world-
wide distribution. Even Allen, surely one of the
most lucid of authors on the subject, refers to
Miller's as the "latest" classification. Since 1940
there has been only one inclusive publication exclusively dedicated to the Chiroptera of both
worlds as a single unit: a splendid work by Professor Martin Eisentraut of the Stuttgart Museum,
in 1957. Eisentraut's is the latest and most complete listing of genera, but it still appears to be a
compilation derived from Anderson, Simpson,
and, as always, Miller. And so Miller yet survives.
Allen chose to group Miller's seventeen families
in tabular form, emphasizing these major groups,
(1) Old World families, (2) New World families, and (3) families common to both hemispheres. I can imagine no more clear approach,
but Allen's listing does not include subfamilies,
which, I believe, are a help toward a more lucid
identity. The following charts include subfamilies
and only roughly indicate the numbers of genera;
certain of the latter being, still, subjects of intense
controversial opinion.

These are names now more or less familiar to us.
I chose not to list by name under hemispheric
distribution until we had learned at least some
significant characteristics of separation in comparing one with another. We know that in numerous cases there are a great many genera or
"kinds," say, of the horsehoe *Hipposideridae* or
among the giant *Pteropodidae*. These are further
separated, of course, into species and subspecies.
We know that some families, such as the *Mys-*

tacinidae, consist of only a single genus and single species. We have discussed the ubiquitous *Vespertilionidae* and, briefly, the free-tailed and sheath-tailed bats which are also at home in both worlds. And we have discussed in part, at least, some few of the hypotheses concerning how they all came to be distributed as they are.

The "two worlds" of which we speak, the Old and the New, are aptly named. They were first so named, one forced upon the other, by the discovery of the American continents in the fifteenth century; before that, square, hexagonal, flat, or round, there was only *the* world. But the New was new only in relation to the Old. Discoveries since that time have led to the conclusion that the New World is indeed *new;* that the Old World, from every evidence thus far unearthed, was, if not the progenitor, then certainly the predecessor of the New. As the warm East has come to be thought of as the birthplace of Man, so also is it seen most likely that all mammals, including bats, had their beginnings there. As Allen relates, "It is clear that most bats are essentially warm-country animals." Their principal home remains in the tropics, and it is likely it has always been so. Any migration out of the Torrid Zone has been an adaptive arrangement over a period of many years, the causes of which can only be illuminated, at best, by an educated guess.

It is presumed by some that such isolated families as the leaf-nosed *Phyllostomatidae* in tropical America are really remnants—though flourishing remnants—of an original ancestral stock which has since died out everywhere else. In such a situation the implication is that the opportunity to develop has gone on unhindered for many millions of years; ample time for successive offshoots

CHART II

OLD WORLD BATS

(excluding the Flying Foxes)

SUBORDER

Microchiroptera

FAMILIES	SUBFAMILIES	COMMON NAMES	APPROX. NUMBERS OF GENERA
Vespertilionidae	*Miniopterinae*	(Bent-winged bat)	1
	Murininae	(Insectivorous Tube-nosed bat)	1
	Kerivoulinae	(Painted bats)	2
	Nyctophilinae	(Big-eared bats)	2
	Vespertilioninae	(Simple-nosed bats)	22
Emballonuridae	*Emballonurinae*	(Sheath-tailed bats)	11
Molossidae	none	(Free-tailed bats)	9
Megadermatidae	"	(False Vampire; "cannibal" bats)	4
Rhinopomatidae	"	(Mouse-tailed bat)	1
Rhinolophidae	"	(Spear-nosed Horseshoe bat)	1
Hipposideridae	"	(Horseshoe bats)	7
Nycteridae	"	(Hollow-faced bat)	1
Mystacinidae	"	(Short-tailed bat)	1
Myzopodidae	"	(Sucker-footed bat)	1

CHART III

NEW WORLD BATS

Microchiroptera

FAMILIES	SUBFAMILIES	COMMON NAMES	APPROX. NUMBERS OF GENERA
Vespertilionidae	*Tomopeatinae* *Vespertilioninae* *Nyctophilinae*	(Peruvian bat) (Simple-nosed bats) (Big-eared bat)	1 12 1
Molossidae	none	(Free-tailed bats)	6
Emballonuridae	*Emballonurinae* *Diclidurinae*	(Sheath-tailed bats) (White Sheath-tailed bat)	7 1
Phyllostomatidae	*Chilionycterinae* *Phyllostominae* *Carolliinae* *Sturnirinae* *Glossophaginae* *Phyllonycterinae* *Stenoderminae*	(Leaf-chinned bats) (Typical Leaf-nosed bats) (Tri-colored Short-tailed Fruit bat) (American Epaulet Fruit bat) (Nectar-feeding Leaf-nosed bats) (Nectar-feeding Small Leaf-nosed bats) (Broad-faced Fruit bats)	3 14 1 1 9 3 8
Noctilionidae	none	(Fish-eating bat)	1
Natalidae	"	(Long-legged bats)	4
Furipteridae	"	(Smoky bats)	2
Desmodontidae	"	(Vampire bats)	3
Thyropteridae	"	(Disc-winged bat)	1

in other parts of the world to originate, prosper, retrogress, die out, and, at last, to sink into oblivion.

The Long-legged *Natalidae*, the Disc-winged *Thyropteridae*, and the Smoky *Furipteridae*, all distantly related, are remnants which, unlike the thriving Leaf-nosed family, are only barely holding their own. Some, within a few thousand, a few hundred years, or possibly even within our own lifetime, as a result of disease or the arrival upon the scene of an unnatural enemy, may see the fragile link of these remnants parted forever.

The ultra-highly specialized fish-eating *Noctilionidae* and the blood-drinking *Desmodontidae* may not only survive but, like the English sparrow, actually thrive under the increasingly preemptive rights of man's dominion. On the other hand, with the slightest falling out of favor—such as in campaigns against rabies—whole groups may be seen to wither and die out within comparatively few years.

Of the Old World families, the larger can reasonably be expected either to continue in their niches or to find new niches. They have the advantage of the old cliché, "nothing makes for success like success." Poor old *Mystacina* of New Zealand, however, and Africa's Sucker-footed *Myzopoda* are not unlikely to be but hanging on a thread. The New Zealand Short-tailed bat is near extinction at the present time because of inroads upon its natural habitat.

Those bats which are common to both major land masses are the Simple-nosed *Vespertilionidae*, the Sheath-tailed *Emballonuridae*, and the Free-tailed *Molossidae*. The *Vespertilionidae* are so varied and numerous it would take an entire book to cover the known scope of their distribution and complicated interrelationships. Their variance in color and in form would seem to be affected not only by minor specialization and difference in habits but by topographic and climatic variations as well. They are our only Temperate Zone bats. The others, the *Emballonuridae* and *Molossidae*, are tropical or subtropical. It can be guessed that their entrance into the New World was by the same route, but not at the same time, as the arrival of the *Phyllostomatidae* or, perhaps, unlike the Leaf-nosed bats, their stamina was such as to continue their progress in both hemispheres.

We have covered the subject of distribution only in such a way as to divide one major group from another. We have not covered the thousand and one details of food sources, topographical hazards, widths of water passages in relation to flight time, the prevalence of wind and storm cycles, and the like. There are simply too many parts of the earth for it to be feasible to cover more than a small area at a time. In a later chapter we shall discuss some of these things.

Having spoken of the world as a whole I would like before leaving this subject to consider briefly, but more practically perhaps, the case of distribution in bats from a political rather than a geographical approach. After all, one never travels to the "Neotropical Zone" or to a "group of islands west of the continental Eurasian land mass"; one goes to "Panama," "England," "Java," or "Peru." It is often difficult to view with an unprejudiced eye the fact that it is we who are the strangers in such places. There are often people of every cast and color, talking gibberish; there are strange noises in the night, and strange bed-fellows in the form of unsolicited insects; and, worse than any of it, no plumbing. On top of it, you say, you cannot identify the birds or animals even if they stop long enough for you to have a look at them. But if we stop to consider that our approach may be wrong, that these are natural things going about their business in a place which is natural to them, we will see more and suffer less.

A "Bat Handbook," as such, considering the numbers of people who would be clamoring at the bookstores and innundating the publisher with frantic demands for copies, would seem an unlikely business investment. A "Guide to the Bats of Uzbekistan, U.S.S.R.," would hold little interest unless one were an Uzbekistanian with a broken-down tractor and nothing else to do. But which of us who has traveled has not wished for some kind of handbook to tell us about the things he saw? Not always, but generally, it is after we get there that we think of these things.

In nearly every country foreign to us there are adequate or near-adequate books to help us. Even if we cannot read a word of the language there is usually some kind of accompanying picture. Books on mammals do not always have chapters on bats, but such books usually do, and one can also obtain a great deal of interesting information from local people who (suddenly awakened to pride of possession) will tell you in detail of the local fauna.

The world is indeed round and—rockets or no rockets—it remains that way. We may consider bats which coinhabit our world to be subordinate in numbers of things, but whatever their role the fact remains they are distributed over the face of the earth with no less of calculable direction than are we.

8

Wired for Sound

From where I am sitting I can see, through gaps in the nearly naked trees, the mirrored reflection in a tidal estuary of what appears to be an observatory. It stands on a hill and its dome is bright in the morning sun. But it is not an observatory, or at least it is not one of the celestial variety. It is a radar installation—a military device made necessary by the times in which we live. If the wind is right one hears from time to time minor creakings and occasional odd noises; noises faint and in no way disturbing, but foreign to our quiet woods.

Radar is a "radio detection device which sends out a powerful beam of high-frequency electromagnetic waves." We knew that much from the dictionary as soon as we heard of radar in its early stages. Its use during World War II is well known; it is known that it is yet with us as a comforting protective device; and it is also fairly generally accepted that bats had at least something to do with its discovery. All of which is true but the last. Bats had nothing to do with it, unless perhaps in some small part of man's inspiration. Further, the terms of reference, "radar" and "sonar," are intermixed with such abandon as to confuse the two completely. Popularly, radar is considered to be somehow "sent through the air," while sonar is believed to be more or less the "underwater equivalent." Actually, the two are separated by the fact that if they make use of actual sound waves they are sonar, and if they utilize electromagnetic waves the process is named radar. Water or air, as such, has nothing to do with it.

Bats, of course, do not have sonar any more than birds have jet engines. Man invented sonar, a highly intricate system of coordinated electronics. But bats—certain bats—do have a sense which in many ways is similar. Certainly the bat came first, and man will admit to having considered the bat in his efforts to perfect his machine; but it would be erroneous to give the credit to the bat, for man, at first, had to go his way alone. Knowledge that bats had a similar system was brought to light nearly simultaneously with man's discovery. Now, years later, the bat is being used to help perfect more advanced types of radar and sonar devices.

Those bats most highly developed in this unique attribute of being "wired for sound" are mainly the insect-eating varieties. The greater number of the Vespertilionidae, the Hipposideridae, Emballonuridae, and Phyllostomatidae, and, in fact, most of the bats outside the fruit-eating variety and the extremists in specialized food habits, are in some way provided with exterior equipment to enhance their sensory perception. The most obvious are those bats with greatly enlarged ears and nose-leaves; these are functionally adept in every way but no more so than the ultra-conservative *Myotis*, who, although drab in comparison to the more exotically designed types, is nonetheless an equally good insect trap. What these bizarre "extras" do, then, is to enhance, to greater or lesser degree, the capabilities of individual genera. Obviously some need them, others do not.

These kinds of bats have long been with us, as we have learned from our brief review of fossil species. Man has known about bats through every stage of his development, since from earliest times bats and man have been coinhabitants of the same fissures, caves, and finally, houses. It would seem that man would have known bats more intimately than other mammals. Oddly enough, that does not seem to have been the case, but it is not surprising that as man advanced into more complicated matters than food and shelter he would leave the bears and other such food products behind and come to consider the functioning of less mundane animals.

It took a long time. Not until 1794 did man stop viewing the bats with less of a superstitious or philosophic approach and turn to them the hard and critical eye of science. In that year, Lazzaro Spallanzani, an Italian, somehow overcome with curiosity about how bats and other night-flying creatures could fly in the darkness, began experimenting with owls and bats. He found that total darkness defeated the owl but not the bat. In studying the structure of the eye he could still find no answer, so he resorted to blinding several bats. He found that even deprived of their sight, they could avoid such obstacles as silk threads which he had arranged to bisect a room obliquely. Going further, Spallanzani released the blinded bats to see if there was a possibility of their being able to return to the tower from which he originally obtained them. Some days later he discovered the blind bats back among the others in the colony, and found, upon dissecting specimens of each, that the stomachs of the blind bats were as full as those which were normal. These experiments, Spallanzani reasoned, showed only that bats need not rely on their eyes, but, it was only after he made repeated experiments that he came to the conclusion the ears played an important role in nocturnal flight. He found that plugging up the ears made the bats helpless and unplugging them immediately restored them to a state of normality. But this only served to make matters worse: "How," he thought, "can ears replace sight?" How can ears alone explain their stomachs being filled with flying insects? There seemed to be no answer. Despite every kind of experiment and the most carefully drawn theories, the problem remained unanswered. Spallanzani died in 1799.

Over a hundred years passed. There had been intermittent attempts at further experimentation but no new discovery was made and "Spallanzani's bat problem" remained. In the early 1900s Rollinat and Trouessart, in France, and Walter Hahn in the United States, began making more careful experiments. They arranged for more complicated mazes through which bats were made to pass, and recorded all details with painstaking accuracy. Hahn went even further by amputating the ears and tragus, but still the bats flew with ease through the maze. It was then established that the inner ear, and not the external appendage, held the answer.

There were other experiments, now mainly concentrated on the inner ear. Plugs were again brought into use, as they had been a hundred years before. By using plaster plugs, which were hard but through which some sound could be heard, it was found the percentage of accurate flights was drastically reduced; also, by using Vaseline, and thus covering up any exposed nerve endings, further percentages of inaccuracies were recorded.

Interested scientists continued to worry Spallanzani's old problem as a dog worries a bone, but nothing new was disclosed. In the late 1930s, Glover Allen prepared a paper under a grant from Harvard University which was published as a semipopular book in 1940. Even at that late date, Allen said, in evaluating Hahn's work, "No doubt it is the echo of vibrations set in motion by air currents that they really perceive."

At the same time, the late 1930s, a young student at Harvard began experimenting with bats on a plane which had previously been considered but as many times discarded: the possibility that bats make sounds in addition to those well-known, i.e., ultrasonic sounds, beyond human perception. With the help of the physics department at Harvard and the Massachusetts Institute of Technology, Donald R. Griffin became the first to break through the old problem instigated by Spallanzani; the high-pitched clicks by which bats navigate were observed and recorded for the first time.

The breakthrough by Griffin was nearly simultaneous with that made by technicians in echolocation, the nucleus of those devices which, when perfected, became known as sonar and radar. Scientists had periodically considered bats as a possible source in solving problems of navigation. As early as 1912, after the *Titanic* disaster, efforts were made to find some means of penetrating darkness and fog. Nearly everyone so employed occasionally thought of bats, but with each consideration there was a quickly followed disavowal of the idea. As Griffin has since said, "Had scientists been less scornful of bats and had they known more about Spallanzani's 'bat problem' more progress would have been made."

The results are now known: sonar and bats function on the same principle. This principle is simply that sounds being sent out from a given source are returned to that source in the sequence in which they collide with opposing objects. As with a flashlight pointed into the blackness of a summer night, there is no return of the beam unless it "hits" a low cloudbank or the branches of a tree; it simply "disappears" (as far as we are concerned) unless returned by an object.

Sounds, then, do indeed go out from our bats; sounds generally beyond the range of human ears, but nonetheless as good, solid, and complete sounds as those of a forceful baritone at the Metropolitan Opera. It has been estimated in fact, that the sound a bat makes, measured a few inches from its mouth, registers as much intensity "as the roar of a four-jet airliner a mile away" (McCue). The sounds are made quite as "loudly" then, but on a different scale, so that their noisiness goes undetected. These sounds are not a prolonged screech but rather a long series of individual clicks or "beeps," which have been counted at 250 to the second. And, these beeps are not always transmitted in a steady, single pitch, but, like FM radio signals, the frequency is "modulated" or altered, starting at 100,000 cycles per second as the animal "cruises" but scaling down to 30,000 cycles or even to 16,000 or less as he zeroes in on his target. Approximately 16,000 cycles per second is the limit audible to the most perceptive human ear, and, since at certain times a bat's voice descends to this range, upon occasions what Griffin calls a "very fast ticking" is audible to humans. Those who work with bats in their sound laboratories theorize that variations in these sliding frequencies may enable individual bats to recognize their own sounds even in a cave full of other bats. Such is a bat's "transmitter."

The "receiver" employed by bats consists of the nose-leaves and/or outer ears as directional finders and amplifiers, the inner ear as a "booster," and, finally, the tiny brain as a nearly instantaneous computer to sort, file, and transmit signals of action. In hundredths of a second the information is received, analyzed, and acted upon. It has been found, by those studying the flight of bats, that they judge range exactly as does sonar, i.e., by computing the time delay between the outgoing pulse and the returning echo. For a target six inches from the bat's mouth, McCue found, the time delay from mouth to prey to ear is about one thousandth of a second, and bats deprived of their hearing in but one ear are still capable of a broad sense of direction but are unable to pinpoint an object.

Rhinolophus,
the Spear-nosed bat

But although the basic system is the same, audiosensitive bats differ greatly in the frequencies they use. Some are ultra variables such as the 100,000 to 20,000 cycle modulating range of the Vespertilionid Little Brown bat, *Myotis,* described above. Others, such as the *Rhinolophidae* and *Hipposideridae,* the Horseshoe bats of the Old World, have a far more simple arrangement: a single frequency (varying from 60,000 to 120,000 cycles depending on the species) which is virtually stable and without modulation. Also, Moehres, the German zoologist, has said that the odd "spear" of which we have spoken in *Rhinolophus* serves to concentrate the sound waves emitted by these bats on the horseshoe-shaped (megaphonelike) excrescence which surrounds the nos-trils. These bats have also a relatively long "beep" which, although lasting only but a fraction of a second—varying from 100 to 50 milliseconds (Griffin)—is still longer in comparative duration. Still other bats, certain neotropical genera such as *Desmodus*, the blood-drinking vampire, and some of the fruit-eating types, have been found to have a far more brief interval of sound, lasting from "only a fraction of a millisecond to 2 or 3 milliseconds." The frequencies employed by these last types vary from as low as 10,000 cycles (well within the range of the human ear) to as high as 150,000 cycles. Also, these tropical bats employ a far more subdued amplitude of sound than the more strident "chirping" varieties.

Exhaustive scientific procedure has proved to us that the theories on echolocation are undeniably true. There are photographs in series to prove that this is so. But how are we to know how the bat can tell an edible flying insect from, say, a totally inedible object such as a pebble thrown into the air? Apparently they cannot judge at a distance the exact nature of the missile, whether it be animal or mineral. They "give chase" in nearly every case but, upon reaching the object, are able to accept or reject it according to their judgment of it. They have not been seen actually to test foreign objects by biting at them (although they often appear to observers to do so), but they will mistake a foreign object for something edible, then be seen to reject it. As our bat cruises, then,

without anything exciting showing on his "radar
screen," his pitch is exceptionally high (more cycles per second) but his "beeps" of sound are
given only at a rate of 10 to 20 per second (comparable, in Griffin's words, to "the slow putt-putt-
putt of a lazy old gasoline engine"). As the bat
picks up a "blip" on his receiver (something in
the way of his own fanning-out of pure sound),
his pitch is lowered while his sound pulse is greatly
accelerated. And in closing with the object this
ratio is even more widely expanded, the frequency often dropping to a low within range of
human hearing, while the emission rate of pulses
is increased to as high as 250 cycles per second
(virtually a high-pitched scream in which individual beeps are lost).

But does the individual insect set up a recog-
nizable sound pattern of its own? Yes, and apparently experience teaches the bat a given number of "old friends," much as we are able to tell
the approximate distance, direction, height, and
state of irritability of certain birds simply by hearing their calls. The insect sends out emanations
peculiar to itself: variations of wing beat and the
molding and general nature of the body and wings,
all having an effect on the pressure put upon the
air in order to set waves of it in motion and regis-
ter as "sound." It was at first thought that bats
located their prey by "hearing" individual sounds
given off by the insect itself. All of this would
enter into it in ratio with the bat's ability to understand or at least recognize its adversary. But
the principle itself is not in "hearing" as such,
but in the returning of the bat's own sound,
"echolocation."

From Spallanzani to the present day observers
have been devising means of gauging the precision

of bats. At first their interest was *can* the bat do it; then, having learned that he could, to what degree, they asked, could he either avoid an obstacle or pinpoint an object. Research is still going on. I have done none of this myself, not even in the most simple arrangement of wires. Having lived with much intimacy with various types of bats in the field, and having seen what they could do, I was disinclined to carry it further. This feeling stemmed not from a lack of desire to do so but from the fact that others had done so much. The field has advanced far beyond the simple wire-stretching stage into advanced electronics, mathematics, and ultra-high-speed photography. Beginning with Griffin, now a professor of zoology at Harvard, the studies have progressed to considerable degree. There is even a large program under way sponsored by the country's Combined Armed Forces. The Lincoln Laboratory, located at Massachusetts Institute of Technology is engaged, under Air Force contract, in studying the intricacies of bat signals with an eye toward possible advancement of knowledge in the field of electronics.

The first inquiries began with the setting up of simple devices to act as barriers to flight. One by one these barriers were increased in difficulty of passage and ratios were set up to judge the comparison of one type of bat with another. The results, after experiments with numerous gauges and angles of wires, were in accordance with the ratio of difficulty, of course, but still the bats continued to penetrate the mazes with a remarkable degree of accuracy. The scientists even resorted to "jamming" i.e., setting up relays of alternate frequencies of competitive sounds. Of course it is known that the bat flies, in nature, through competitive sounds, and perhaps it was to be expected that some answer had been devised in order to overcome the problem. And, of course, "the smallest wire detected in noise was greater than the smallest wire detected in quiet" (Griffin). But it remains remarkable that such a tiny brain, however intricate, is able to shuffle and decipher data in time to react to such complexities of interference. No answer is attempted by any of those at work on this project. No one knows the answer. And, as Griffin states, "We cannot even be sure we are asking the proper questions."

Recent advances in photographic techniques have brought out another interesting sidelight in the continual search by bats for their prey. This is in regard to their methods of actually capturing it. It was long thought that bats simply outflew and "snatched" at their aerial prey, as a dog will jump and snatch at a bone. High-speed camera equipment in the charge of Dr. Frederic A. Webster at the Lincoln Laboratory at Massachusetts Institute of Technology developed the fact that at least some types of bats (in this case *Myotis*), instead of catching their prey in their teeth, actually "field" them in their interfemoral membrane, much as a baseball player fields a ball in his glove. The tail was seen to curl under, thus cupping the membrane as near contact was made with the insect. At the point of actual contact the insect would be held in the cupped membrane for a fraction of time, then the animal would bend over and grasp the insect in its teeth.

Facing page:
Time sequence
of Horseshoe bat
catching a moth
(*After photograph by
Frederic A. Webster*)

Through the kindness of Drs. Griffin and Webster I was invited to Cambridge, Massachusetts, to observe the entire range of experiments through which these hitherto unknown facts were recorded.

I saw the bat (a native Little Brown *Myotis*) taken from its cage and released. An unfrightened bat does not "flutter" or fly erratically; this bat flew with unhurried precision in a continuous elliptical arc a few feet over our heads. The laboratory is built with a high ceiling and has a large trough of shallow water on the floor. The bat was silent as he flew—at least to our ears. But when Dr. Webster switched on an electronic system the "silent" bat was found to be as animated in voice as he was in body. The same system which sent his voice over an amplified speaker also set in motion an oscilloscope which visually portrayed the sounds on a screen. Simultaneously, a battery of electronic flashlighting devices and high-speed cameras recorded every movement as the bat flew into a "target area" along his normal flight path.

As I watched in wonder this remarkable demonstration of coordinates, Dr. Webster proceeded with further experiments as the bat made pass after pass. Small pellets of simulated insect, e.g., pellets of nylon of different dimensions, small bits of wire, etc., were systematically tossed into the target area. The bat would accept or reject the objects according to the degree of its resemblance to its known prey. Each pass and reaction was faithfully recorded and as often photographed. I was particularly amazed to be able actually to hear the amplified sounds as I followed every movement with my eyes. The sounds I heard as the bat

Bat drinking

flew by in his patient elliptical course were "hunting noises," i.e., a regular succession of moderately ranged clicks. As the pellet or mealworm was thrown, these clicks began to accelerate at a vast rate as he zeroed in. Near the actual point of contact the clicks were a virtual scream as in a Geiger counter gone mad. Then, at contact, if the missile was edible there would be, of course, a full mouth and a drastically reduced click pattern; the clicks falling off into Griffin's slow outboard-motor category.

I could detect nothing of the actual catch. It looked as though the prey were simply caught in the mouth. Innumerable pictures entirely disproved such a possibility, as those given me by Dr. Webster plainly indicate. The prey is either caught in the tail membrane or, most frequently, is "fielded" by a wing tip, maneuvered or knocked into the interfemoral membrane, and is then picked up in the mouth.

The drinking process was also revealed as I watched. The bat, having made innumerable passes and captures, was seen to fly lower and lower arcs until he was just skimming the water surface. Quite swallowlike, a lower pass was made, and the water was taken by mouth in full flight. A number of passes seemed necessary before an actual "touchdown" on the water was made—as though his echolocatory apparatus had difficulty in finding the exact range at which to "lower jaw." After all, some caution can be understood when it is realized that, in full flight, a slight error in judgment could mean a faceful and a chill dunking.

The experiments made by Drs. Griffin and Webster have led to conclusions about what Griffin so aptly describes as "bumbling bats." Do bats often err in flight and in so doing either "miss" on a pass or, even, collide with an object? Indeed they do. It has been found not only that sick bats and tired bats often miscalculate, but that even bats in good health and in possession of sound faculties upon occasion are clumsy or careless. For one thing, of course, no physiological function is flawless; as surely as constipation slows the eliminative capacity and overstrain hampers vision, the bat's echolocatory ability is vulnerable to misfunctions. Fortunately for the bat, however, such instances are not of frequent occurrence.

Obsessed with sound, I have somehow neglected thus far to mention the other external sensory organs. Do eyes aid or possibly hinder the bat in his nocturnal flight? Since we are discussing the specialized group which is "wired for sound" I think it can be safely said that the eyes are of little importance in those bats coming under this category. They all do indeed see; some see well. But it is doubtful that they use their eyes to much degree in flight. The eyes, under microscopic scrutiny, are small and insignificant, and seem to lack those elements of more extensive dilation, such as are found in the large fruit bats.

How then, goes it with the nose? Are the noses simply foundations for nose-leaves which might aid in sound reception? This is doubtful. Certainly the sonar-sensitive bats seem to be in possession of every faculty of olfaction. Beyond this there is every indication that the sense of smell may be of considerable more use than we know. Many species are provided with glands which possess a or crevices as well as their feces are often per- very strong, musky scent. In addition, their caves meated with the same heavy odor. It is not only conceivable but perhaps indicative that bats may use this scent as a "homing" device. I have often been able to discern the "bat smell" more than a hundred yards from the cave site. Allen mentions the same experience. I do not doubt that a "homing scent" might be a possibility as a secondary aid to returning bats, but such an hypothesis could hardly explain the fact that bats have been released quite far at sea and have returned over many miles of water to their roosting places. I think it more likely that, as with birds, the homing instinct is a calculative process within the brain or inner ear, connected, possibly, with geomagnetic emanations, or, at least, with some process outside the olfactory sense.

The glands of which I speak, however, must have a function of considerable import, considering the variety and consistency of their occurrence. They are common to the *Mega-* as well as the *Microchiroptera*, and differ greatly in location. Some glands are visible as wartlike projections on the lips, forehead, or throat. Others are located at the base of the tail, the elbow or forearm, or even on the membranes themselves. The uses of these glands are not clear, although it seems probable that they would have some connection with sex and breeding.

The actual flight of these bats is greatly varied. Some species seem to flit quite slowly and moth-like, having no apparent direction and seemingly possessed of a great fragility. Others will zigzag and make surprising aerial swoops at what seems a startling rate of speed. Still others will fly arrow-straight. Some are high fliers while others fly low to the ground, weaving in and out of trees. Some fly early in the evening while it seems as yet broad day, while others never venture out until the night is totally dark.

Miller points out that the less proficient fliers have a more simple articulation at the base of the upper arm with the shoulder blade, while strong fliers have an additional knob which, not improbably, adds to the power of their flight. In other families, as for instance, with the tropical *Molossidae*, the fifth finger is much reduced, thus making a much more narrowed wing and giving greater speed. In others, for example the *Hipposideridae*, the fifth finger is quite long, giving a very broad surface to the wing and emphasizing slow flight and rapid movement in turning.

In none of the *Microchiroptera* do we find any claw other than on the thumb and those on the feet. But in many types there is an additional membrane from the first joint of the thumb to the second joint of the index or second finger. Beyond this, there are only two joints on the index finger in all the *Microchiroptera*, with one exception, *Rhinopoma*, the Mouse-tailed tomb bat; in this case a third joint is evident, a fact regarded as evidence of a primitive retention.

We have mentioned the tail in but one instance, that of serving to assist in prey gathering. The tail doubtless is of use in many other ways besides, but no blanket statement can be made concerning it. As we have observed in our initial listing of the *Microchiroptera*, the tail varies from a long, mouselike appendage, a support for a membrane, to, finally, no tail at all. Obviously where it exists it conforms to a purpose, but this is not always evident. Unlike the function in certain arboreal mammals the tail seems not, in bats, to serve as any sort of "rudder." It seems, more than anything else, to act as only a supporting "strut" or batten. It is generally recognized that those bats with no tails are the more primitive, those with shorter tails less so, and long-tailed species complete with the interfemoral "extra sail" the most advanced. With this in mind the very long, membraneless tail of *Rhinopoma* would seem to be not a yet further

Types of tails

mouse-tail *Rhinopoma*

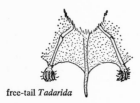

free-tail *Tadarida*

full membrane *Myotis*

sheath-tail *Emballonura*

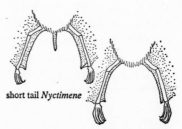

short tail *Nyctimene*

no tail *Pteropus*

advance beyond the Vespertilionid types, but a survival of some long extinct type, possibly a precursor, even, to some of the tailless genera.

As to the kinds of flying insects eaten by the bat who possesses all this glory of ears, eyes, wings, and tail, it would be impossible for me to say. I have taken mosquitoes, flies, ants, moths, nerve-winged insects, and beetles from a host of little stomachs, but seldom are they in such a state that even an expert could identify them. They are more nearly a "mush" if not just a watery gruel if taken from the stomach; but often these bats, upon being shot, will retain some part of the captured prey in their mouths. It would not be too far from the truth to say that bats will eat nearly any flying insect of appropriate size and which has been found to "taste good." The last may sound puerile, except that certain lesser animals and insects have definitely been found to have an unpleasant taste, and, although a bat is not an epicure it takes little charity to give him credit for rejecting something he has found to be unpalatable.

We, the human race, have made extraordinary advances in the fields of technology. Whose young child will not laugh at the simplicity, too well apparent, of early radio? We are so chock-a-block filled with "high fidelity," "woofers" and "tweeters," and the omnipresent idiocy of the television box, that anything less complex seems old-fashioned. And we are right, I presume; the world is moving, and moving with it, I suppose, we have the right of priority to jeer playfully at those left behind. Truly enough, we may have no more to learn from the bat whom we may seem to have left behind. Scientists do not think this is true, however. They believe we have a great deal yet to learn.

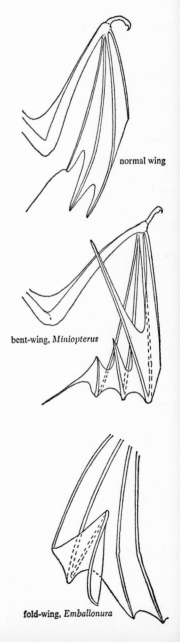

normal wing

bent-wing, *Miniopterus*

fold-wing, *Emballonura*

9

Giants
in Paradise

On a warm afternoon in June of the year 1770, Captain Cook's ship *Endeavor* was careened on the wide beach of a river mouth in the north of Australia. Repairs were being made on the hull. The thud of mallets jarred the air and the reek of tar mingled with the pungent, rooty smell of the jungle which bordered the river. A mob of screaming cockatoos catapulted from the high trees into the dwarfed mangroves, causing Joseph Banks to look up from the botanical specimens he had been drying. Cook himself was quietly surveying the outer reefs with his brass telescope, and was undisturbed by the undulations of straw-necked ibis which billowed up then settled back down again in the near mangrove tangle. The smoke from the tar fires rose straight into the air and the sun was warm and soft.

Suddenly, into this tranquil scene burst a running seaman, wildly shouting and gesticulating toward the bush from which he had come. He breathlessly told a strange tale of a most terrible animal, "as black as the devil, and had wings, and about the size of a gallon keg." A scouting party was dispatched and the "devil" was found. It was a "flying fox," to the seaman a most weird and horrifying creature.

So the story goes. . . .

Frankly, I do not believe it. Far before 1770 ships had been going into the Indies, to India and Africa, where fruit bats are common. I think the story, which is, in essence, what I have told, is just so much hokum. But it reads well enough and holds one truth which is most undeniable: to European eyes, meaning our own, the first sight of one of these creatures is a shock. To most of us the sight of a *bat* well over a yard wide circling over our house in the deepening dusk would cause rather more excitement than a Russian satellite. We can talk all we may about the fact that these animals do exist, we can call them *Pteropus* in the most familiar way and look at pictures by the score, but it is not until we actually see them that the real truth of their being comes through. These giants are no bugbear, no "devil-devil" and, really, nothing unusual; that is, nothing unusual within their proper sphere.

Flying foxes are a sure sign of your arrival in the Old World tropics. However hot and humid the days, the tropic nights are cool and soft. The sweet scent of frangipani, the rustle of palm fronds, and the strident scream of the flying fox would tell me, were I totally blind, that I had returned to Paradise. Not all would agree. To many this hot, sweet land is an infestuous "Green Hell." This is not an apologia. The tropics are clearly both these things. My own feeling, as intensely one-sided as most, is one of deep and abiding affection, and the raucous scream of the great flying foxes yet haunts me like a Siren.

We have discussed, in brief, certain morphological details of the *Pteropodidae*. We know that they have very proper eyes, large and bright, in contrast to their sound-sensitive cousins; that they are relatively simple and unadorned exteriorly; and that they subsist mainly on fruit. We have learned that they gather together in camps and that they migrate periodically to follow the fruiting season. But other than these things, what of their nature? How, exactly, do they function, and what are they really like?

It is really quite difficult to try and get at the character of any animal without falling into the trap of anthropomorphizing. After all, the least of animals, from germs upward, are a complex of such forces that they vie with the galaxies and nebulae for sheer incomprehensibility. No one really "understands" any animal; they are to be contemplated in relation to other things or animals only by specific points of difference. The word "intelligent" used to describe an animal is the most useless of words. We all use it. I use it now: I will say that I think certain of the *Pteropodidae* are "intelligent." I say it, knowing better. They are really not, I am certain; but they seem so. They seem so in relation to one's contact with them.

I have spoken before of how one might hold a bat in the hand in order to become on terms of intimacy. With flying foxes this would not, obviously, be sound advice. For one thing, certainly, they would not at all fit in the hand, and for another, if the hand were brought into it, it would no doubt be soundly bitten, for the teeth of these bats are proportionately far longer than those of the canine quadrupeds after whom they are named. The reason behind this striking quality of being "long in the tooth" lies not in the rending of flesh but in the use of the teeth more as "can openers," for surely a coconut, for the uninitiated, presents as nearly impenetrable a façade as anything outside a bank vault. For a coconut one must be prepared—and the flying fox most certainly is; his teeth are long and as sharp as an awl.

The fur is seldom silky in quality as with many of the *Microchiroptera*; rather, it is generally coarse and often somewhat frizzled. But this seeming defect is more than compensated for by the color, which is very often of a rich and bright hue. I do not mean "bright" as with birds, but I do mean quite bright as far as mammals go: the yellows are often toward the orange spectrum and the browns are not dull and muted but shadings of rich mahoganies and shining umbers. And, as often as not, such colors are placed so as to be in direct contrast, one complementing the other.

But it is neither teeth nor fur nor even size which most captures my imagination in these bats; it is their eyes. The eyes are usually quite large and often light brown rather than dark umber or black; upon occasion even, they are a rich amber. It is not the color, however, which has moved me, but the remarkable quality of wonder which their eyes suggest. I have had captive, over the years, some hundreds of kinds of animals of one type or another. In the eyes of all one could read varying messages. Certainly fear is always the most pronounced reaction and is readily to be seen in nearly every captive. But in some there is to be seen the piercing stare of black anger; in others a sort of confused acceptance. I will swear that in dolphins I have seen a true intelligence shine through. But with the giant flying foxes the one feeling I have above all others is that the captive animal does not really believe that *I* am real! The look of sheer wonder seems to surmount even the natural wall of fear. I have never seen a more truly "fish out of water" look; as though its little brain could only send back a message of thorough disbelief to the wondering eyes. I would call it a look of the most pure innocence. I always feel that I have trod at last on some threshold we were not meant to cross. But what one feels is a personal matter and hardly one which might have any effect whatever on the bat. As a matter of fact, I would say that even the most scientific of inquiries into what any mammal—other than ourselves—actually thinks or feels is so equivocal in substance as to be hardly worth noting; that is, of course, until it has passed from theory into experimentally proved reaction beyond dispute.

Quite aside from color, size, or cast, bat's eyes are remarkable. It is no strain on our imagination to perceive that the eyes of bats are myopic and insensitive as well as being minute. Whether these eyes have retrogressed or have merely never grown to be, we do not know. With some bats, however, and the flying fox are included among these, eyes are a decidedly important factor in the functioning structure of the animal. When we see the great, yellow, dilated orbs of an owl we are not surprised that the bird can navigate through the darkness. Fruit bats have not these saucerlike objects, yet they too, seem at home in the dark. This problem so fascinated a German named Walter Kolmer that he microscopically studied the eyes of many kinds of animals in comparison with those of others, among which were sixteen genera of fruit bats compared with an equal number of the *Microchiroptera*. His findings produced the

Rousettus,
a Fruit bat

amazing information that, although the giant bats had not eyes the size of an owl's, they had an equally remarkable structure unlike any other type of eye. He found that the retina is quite different from other animals', possessing many small villi-like capillary endings which project like mounds on the outer layers of the retina. On these projections are some thirty thousand or so little nerve endings, each of which evidently acts as a tiny light-perceptive cell. The effect, because of these projections, is that the surface area is far greater than would be the retina of the usual concave flat surface. It can be presumed that the fruit bats, because of this adaptation, are possibly among those animals which see best in the darkness, although no facts are as yet known in this regard.

It is also thought that bats are totally color-blind. Here again, Kolmer tells us that many diurnal animals have, in company with the rodlike nerve endings, a great number of cone-shaped cells which hold small grains. These are thought to be the source of color perception. Since the fruit bats seem totally to lack these types of cones it is deduced that they lack color perception of any kind.

But one thing more: Can these bats with eyes seemingly unparalleled for nocturnal vision, see in the total darkness of a deep cave beyond the reach

Dobsonia,
the Spinal-winged
Flying Fox

of even faint starlight? I doubt it. Few of the flying foxes are cave bats, for one thing, and for another, those which are usually frequent the outer
recesses of caves. Beyond that—and this would
seem most pertinent—the only fruit bat which
does frequent the darkest parts of caverns, *Rousettus*, has been proved the single exception in
the entire family thus far known that possesses a
form of audioreception akin to the *Microchiroptera*. It is interesting to note that E. Kulzer however, records that the sounds in *Rousettus* come
not from the larynx but from the tongue, much
after the fashion, as Griffin suggests, of sounds
like the "human vocal clicks usually written 'tsk,
'tsk." Griffin goes on to state that this adaptation
in *Rousettus* is suggestive of having been developed long after the divergence of the *Mega-* from
the *Microchiroptera*; somewhat as an afterthought
in order to adapt to a single niche in evolutionary
trend, not on a swing one way or the other.

The *Pteropodidae* appear to be far more than
the term "firm of flesh" would seem to indicate.
Perhaps it is because of their rather shorter fur,
but they seem muscularly gigantic. No one holding a dead specimen can but be impressed: first of
all with the weight—often over two or three
pounds—and secondly, with the four great back
and breast muscles which operate its flying mechanism. Now, when one holds a bird in the same
manner, one *expects* it to be able to fly. The body
always seems rather more light than we would
have supposed enough to insure flight. Even with
the smaller bats one finds the suggestion of speed
and lightness. But with the flying foxes, even
though the wings are expansive and impressive,
still, there is no tail or stabilizing membrane as in
other bats, and the weight seems so oddly dispro-

Facing page:
Pteropus neohibernicus,
among world's largest
bats

Nyctimene,
the Tube-nosed
fruit bat

portionate as to make flight unlikely. One im-
agines that, without either tail or membrane, the
animal must surely be front-heavy and must continually be bracing itself for an ignominious nose
dive. But although in flight they are not as buoy-
ant as other species, they seem quite stable indeed
and fly with a well-oiled precision. Their flight is
slow but steady, suggestive, to those who have a
knowledge of birds, of the heavy-bodied Great
Horned owl. The flight, also like the owl's, is
silent, except in times of abrupt changes in course,
when their great wings, overworking to avoid a
collision, pound the air in such a manner as to
sound like one furiously beating the brim of a felt
hat.

As one who shamelessly admits to standing in
city streets with head thrown back in amazement
when an airplane passes over, perhaps then, I am
childishly left behind you who have accepted
these things as commonplace. Perhaps by now I
should have learned, but the wonder yet remains.
Birds, one feels, *should* fly, and bats, as well, are
supplied with "wings" and one is not surprised to
see them together in the air of an early evening,
one going home to roost and the other (one can
imagine a lunch pail clattering) going off on the
"night shift." But the resemblance ends there.

Bird (top),
Bat (bottom)

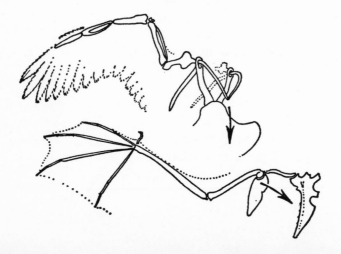

Structurally, far beyond divisions of biological reproduction and external features, there are extreme differences in their make-up for venturing into the same element. Birds are powered by two large breast muscles on either side of a deep keel of bone. The inner muscle raises the wing while the outer pulls it down, giving cause, as the ratio of wing raisings and lowerings overbalance the weight of the body, for the whole parcel of machinery—bill, breast, feathers, claws, and all—to rise on a cushion of air. A bit of lowering of the tail and adjustment of pitch in wings and there is both a rising and a going forward. We might do much the same things with a pair of fans held in each hand, were the ratio of body weight to fans, plus power, switched round to a different order—which sounds quite silly except that that is exactly what has happened in the bat. The principal difference, flightwise, is the lack, in bats, of the deeply keeled breastbone. The bird has virtually no back muscles: the wing-raising is done by a tendon which serves the same purpose as a downhaul on a sailboat; by passing through a block, the leverage is executed in reverse, that is, reverse actions are handled from the one spot. In bats there are "top muscles" and "bottom muscles"—each doing its job after the fashion of the old railway handcar. Actually, from the point of

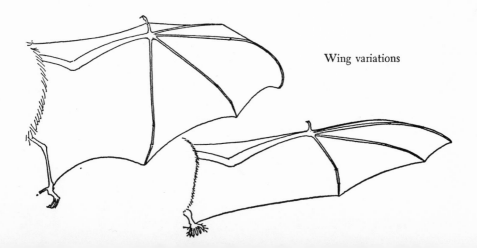

Wing variations

simple mechanics, the bat's arrangement is more simple, direct, and capable of moving a greater mass than the more complicated avian principle. Which is as it should be; greater weights in ratio are necessary to lift the mammal than are required for the bird. Of course, were the arrangement of tendons doubled back in birds, we would have use of the principle evident in a block and tackle, where the ratio is drastically multiplied to permit the carriage of far greater weights than would ordinarily be possible. As it is, however, as anyone knows who has tried to free a topsail block or raise a mainsail without benefit of a winch, it is infinitely more direct to have someone else pulling from the top.

I have mentioned that the canine teeth are long and sharp. Their work is the tearing of husks and virtually ends there. The molar teeth in most of the *Pteropodidae* are very flattened to allow for the grinding and crushing of fruit pulp. In *Nyctimene* the canines are strangely blunt and notched. Some of the *Macroglossinae*, or Nectarfeeders, in addition to their extraordinarily long tongues, have teeth and an extremely thin lower jaw which evidently aid in their specialized feeding.

Much has been mentioned from time to time about the sense of smell in bats, and, in particular,

Muscle structure

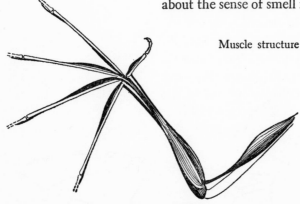

about that sense in the fruit bats. Australian fruit growers to whom I have talked, as well as field observers who would seem to know, have strongly opined that the flying foxes, for all their visual good sense, are undoubtedly guided to orchards and other sources of fruit through their sense of smell. Troughton relates that apiarists have found that when the air is charged with the sweet odor of separated honey, fruit bats are drawn in great numbers. Also, bitten fruit and windfalls, their aroma released, are a source of considerable attraction. I know nothing by my own experience of these possibilities, but I think it not unlikely that it is true.

The kind of fruit eaten by these bats depends upon where the individual is located, and "fruit" has so vague a meaning that in itself it means little except that a "fruit-eater," as such, is simply not an eater-of-something-else. Certainly pawpaws are a great favorite, as are figs, both wild and cultivated. Apples, plums, pears, and peaches, as well as guavas, bananas, mangoes, plantains, and breadfruit, are welcomed. Coconuts—the small, succulent, green coconuts—are commonly downed. Citrus fruits are not as well liked, it seems, but will do when all else fails. Berries of many types are consumed as are certain flowers, their nectar and pollen. A most vivid recollection of the flying fox's food habits is one of late evening while I was sitting by a copra shed, rather idly waiting for the tube-nosed *Nyctimene* to come out of an archway of jungle. As I was concentrating on the sweet whistle of *Nyctimene* coming toward me in the darkness, my gun at the ready, *Pteropus*, flying at a great height, dropped a large mango BANG! straight onto that tin roof! The gun went off and I found myself with my nose in the gravel, quak-

ing in every bone. I have not quite got over it yet.

In most species of the flying fox—at least in those known—there is only one breeding season each year, and only one young born and raised. At birth the young bat clings to one of its mother's two teats with small deciduous teeth which are acutely hooked in order to withstand the rigors and contortions of the mother's flight. As the young bat grows heavier it is often left hanging on a nearby tree as the mother flies off and returns with fruit to feed it. Among the genus *Pteropus* the males are generally larger than the females and are often, in flight, to be distinguished from the females by their long, swaying penises, which, because of their large size, look, at times, like dangling tails.

There is never any nest or protective covering sought in the camps. I have often seen them after a morning rain, glistening and steaming under the rays of the bright sun. One comes upon their camps, however, only infrequently; their presence is known more intimately by their coming to you: they are nightly visitants during the fruiting season to any coconut tree. They seem to be among the most quarrelsome of all animals, continually being pushed, flapping and scratching and screaming, from some choice spot on the coconut palm, by another just as strident and just as noisy.

It is supposed that fruit bats have few enemies outside of man. But Troughton, the Australian zoologist, suspects that the large eagles, goannas, crocodiles (which snap them up as they fly down to drink from some pool), and snakes are a greater menace than has previously been thought. As has been said, man both eats them and destroys them as pests, but yet they seem to survive in considerable numbers.

CHART IV: THE FLYING FOXES

SUBORDER

Megachiroptera

FAMILY

Pteropodidae

SUBFAMILY

Pteropodinae

TRIBE	TRIBE	TRIBE	TRIBE
Pteropodini (The Flying Foxes)	Harpyionycterini (The Harpy Fruit bat)	Epomophorini (The Epaulet Fruit bats)	Cynopterini (The Short-nosed Fruit bats)

SUBTRIBE
Rousettina
(Rousette bats)
Rousettus
Eidolon
Myonycteris
Boneia

Harpyionycteris

SUBTRIBE
Pteropodina
(True Flying Foxes)
Pteropus
Neopteryx
Acerodon
Pteralopex
Styloctenium

SUBTRIBE
Dobsoniina
(Spinal-winged
Flying Fox)
Dobsonia

Plerotes
Epomops
Hypsignathus
Epomophorus
Micropteropus
Scotonycteris
Nanonycteris
Casinycteris

SUBTRIBE
Cynopterina
(Short-nosed Fruit
bats)
Cynopterus
Thoopterus
Balionycteris
Chironax
Dyacopterus
Penthetor
Sphaerias
Ptenochirus
Megaerops
Aethalops
Haplonycteris

SUBTRIBE
Nyctimenina
(Tube-nosed Fruit
bats)
Nyctimene
Paranyctimene

SUBFAMILY

Macroglossinae

TRIBE	TRIBE
Macroglossini (Long-faced Nectar-eating bats) Eonycteris Macroglossus Syconycteris Megaloglossus	Notopterini (Short-faced Nectar-eating bats) Notopteris Melonycteris Nesonycteris

A detailed enumeration of the *Megachiroptera* would seem superfluous perhaps, since we have absorbed segments along the way. But briefly, the suborder *Megachiroptera* contains one family, the *Pteropodidae*, or True Flying Foxes; two sub-families, the *Pteropodinae* or Long-nosed Flying Foxes, the *Macroglossinae*, or Long-tongued Flying Foxes, the first containing four principal Tribes, the *Pteropodini*, the *Harpyionycterini*, the *Epomophorini* and the *Cynopterini*—and the latter containing two Tribes, the *Macroglossini* and the *Notopterini* (see Chart IV). All of these differ greatly in appearance one from the other, but the separations of the genera under each family or subfamily may or may not be obvious to the untrained eye. For instance, *Pteropus* differs greatly from *Dobsonia*, and the African *Epomophorus*, although it looks very unlike *Hypsignathus*, is closely allied to it, while *Macroglossus* and *Syconycteris* are nearly identical in the hand.

You will see in some of the assorted sketches that they do indeed vary considerably; some have tails, some do not; there are long noses and short, the gargantuan and diminutive in size. There is one point, however, in which they do not vary, and it is this point which sets them aside from all other bats. This is the presence, on the index finger, of a distinct claw in addition to that on the thumb. All have it. Lacking it, though flying-fox-like, they are not flying foxes.

Griffin and others prefer Eisentraut's clear-cut "Fledermaus" and "Flughund," obviously "flitter mouse" and "flying dog," for what could be called "common names" for the two major divisions of bats. And actually the *Megachiroptera* do far more resemble the dog rather than the fox. But for me it will always remain flying fox. It was under that name that I first saw them, close by, just over the coconut tops on a hot, scented evening in an April that is now rather long ago. I have seen many since, of varied kinds, but none will ever match in grandeur that first splendid sight.

How large are they? Rather, I might begin at the smaller end. The smallest, the elflike little *Syconycteris* (for an example) is no larger than a *Myotis*, our own Little Brown bat, a mere ball of fur to cup in one's hand. The others are in between. *Epomophorus* is smallish; *Hypsignathus* is certainly largish—up to three feet in wingspread. But how large are the *largest?* There is considerable doubt, still, even among learned mammalogists, about which, exactly, is the greatest bat of them all. Some say that *Pteropus giganteus* of India is the largest, but follow up that statement by saying "nearly five feet" in wingspread. I wish to make no statement of contradiction, for, plainly and simply, I can say I do not know which is the greater in size. But I will say that I have seen bats larger than five feet in wingspread, and I am prepared to prove it by listing the following data:

Pteropus neohibernicus papuanus
From Omsis, near Lae, Territory of New Guinea
July, 1959
AMNH #191214
Total length: 455 millimeters
Forearm: 213   "
Wingspread: 1650   "

Now 1650 millimeters equals exactly five feet, four and fifteen sixteenths inches. That specimen which I note above is to be found in the collection of the American Museum of Natural History in New York. I have collected others of the same species which would have been well over five feet six inches. I strongly feel that the six-foot mark is a possibility so great that I should be willing to wager on its eventual discovery as I unashamedly continue to say that certain bats attain a size of "nearly six feet."

At any rate, they are large, these friends of mine. They are, more or less, "as black as the devil and have wings and are about the size of a gallon keg." All of which brings us back again to where we began.

10

Tigers of
the Air

I am about to discuss with you certain bats whose nature and physiognomy are rather startling and are perhaps, of all their kind, the most dramatic. These are the rapacious "cannibal bats," bats which pursue and devour other bats. *Megadermatidae*, the family name, as you can see, means only "great-skinned." The name means little. One must see this bat for oneself.

I think you will agree with me that there is something impressive about this bat. True, he has not the harlequin atmosphere of certain of the Horseshoe bats, nor does he have, as with the giant flying foxes, a size of any really startling dimension. What he has is a rather forward-leaning dreadful earnestness which bespeaks his occupation. He has, indeed, great ears—but other bats have larger ears. He, too, has a nose-leaf—but we have now seen dozens. What makes him different from other bats is what makes a tiger a tiger. That which thrills the spectators at a circus is not that the trainer is caged with a great, striped, sinuous,

125

shimmering beast; the spectator knows he is caged with Death. The name *Megaderma* alludes in all probability to the large, naked ears. He might better have been named *Mors*, for Death, in the bat world, is exactly what he is.

There is nothing shocking about death in nature. Nature is death, as it is life. We are quick to judge—I think all of us are—whether one act of violence or another is in this or that category. Only last week I overheard a lady—whose shoulders were lately draped with a mink stole—say to her husband concerning a browned and succulent turkey, "Oh, just twist the leg off, Jack." Jack did, and there was not so much as a quiver among the assemblage. Were the same lady faced with killing and plucking that turkey, or to skinning those mink, she would straightaway choose to faint. "Eaters of meat are we!"—who said it? I cannot remember. But it is true. We are eaters of meat, but we are no longer individual killers of meat.

A carnivore is one which devours flesh. Put that way, it is hardly appetizing. But it is true. There is an entire order in the animal world which eats nothing else. That sleeping bundle of fur by your fire is a carnivore. You and I are omnivores— which means, perhaps, that we are less fastidious. Tigers, dogs, and other carnivores—the lot of them—are insistent on their fare and each is an integral cog in the communal job of weeding out the culls from sound stock. No proper dog eats salad.

To those who will say, "Come, come now; back to your subject," I will say that I have never left it. I am not endeavoring to convince you, through some sorcery of words, that tigers and dogs are alike to bats. I do mean to say, again, that we are all here together; inextricably, inseparably welded together, and each is doing his job because he was made that way.

There is more than one carnivorous bat. To be exact, there are four—at least there are four of which I am certain; there may possibly be others. No one knows the full extent of this or nearly any other aspect if it concerns bats, but in this case I refer to "eaters of meat," not insects. In order to prevent confusion I will name these known four in their established order, and tell why other genera in the same families are not to be placed in this category. Three families are known to have carnivorous members: the *Nycteridae*, consisting of but one genus; the *Megadermatidae* whose genera are four, *Megaderma*, *Macroderma*, *Lavia*, and *Cardioderma*; and the *Phyllostomatidae*, among which are the largest of the South American Leaf-nosed bats.

Of the *Megadermatidae*, *Nycteris*, the Hollow-faced bat, is too small for much blood lusting and is a known insect-feeder. *Lavia* and *Cardioderma* are also rather small and are insect-eaters. That leaves *Megaderma*, *Macroderma*, and two genera of the *Phyllostomatidae*, *Vampyrum*, and *Phyllostomus*. Only four, as I say, but I think they will prove well able to satisfy the most sanguine among us.

Megaderma is a southeast Asian genus. The popular name for this bat is False Vampire. As we have learned, such names can lead to little more than confusion; the name "vampire" was based on a myth, and the heir to the dubious title, the true Vampire of Central America, is half a world away and about as different as a bat can be. But no matter. To begin, these bats are among the largest of all the *Microchiroptera*, measuring nearly two feet in wingspread. Their principal external characteristics are the very large and erect ears, joined halfway up on their inner edges, with a divided tragus, long and narrow and erect nose-leaves, and a very short—nearly unrecognizable—tail. They are generally quite pale but the colors vary in intensity between species.

The first recognition of the *Megadermatidae* was in 1810 when Geoffroy published an account in Paris. Undoubtedly the China trade had brought it back as a curiosity. Later, in increasing numbers, naturalists began to accompany trading expeditions and greater numbers of specimens and more knowledge was channeled back to Europe. Among those naturalists was an Edward Blyth who gave one of the first accounts of the extraordinary habits of these bats.

Blyth's story concerned a *Megaderma* which flew into a lighted room in India. In trying to capture it he caused the bat to drop that which he thought was its young. But he found it to be a small insect-eating bat of another species which had a curious bleeding wound behind its ear. Having caged both bats together he was surprised to see the *Megaderma* attack the smaller bat (an Asian Pipistrelle) "fastening on it with the ferocity of a tiger and seizing it behind the ear." The larger bat then proceeded to devour the smaller until nothing was left but the wings and head.

Allen, that indefatigable researcher, quotes Blyth and many others who describe the orgies of these bats. One Colonel McMaster of Rangoon (relates Allen) reported two canaries killed by *Megaderma*. The bat squeezed between the thin wire bars of their cage. Another report describes not only the destruction of bats, but the consumption of frogs. The bat's habit of dining is evidently to fly to the wall of a house with his captives and there dismember them at his leisure, letting the fragments fall to the floor. Occasionally the heads of mice are found and many kinds of small birds. From Ceylon and Burma there are reports of these bats hovering over trees and hunting through shrubs searching out the nestlings of birds. Among the birds it seems to prefer are the little white-eyes, sunbirds, and flower-peckers as particular favorites. Observers from localities where the bats are reasonably abundant describe the sound of dropping parts of bodies as not an uncommon one. Apparently bats, birds, and frogs —it sounds like a dissertation from Aristophanes —are not the only victims of these bats. They are also known to fly up and down walled areas picking up nocturnal lizards and geckos.

Griffin, recognizing the work of Moehres and Kulzer and Novick, describes these bats as "Whispering bats"—bats having pulses of low intensity and short duration. These sounds are often so low that the most delicate of microphones are needed at nearly point-blank range in order to insure amplification. Griffin concludes that the "loud" bats are those which pursue very small gnat-sized flies and mosquitoes. Fruit-eaters (other than the Megachiroptera) such as the Phyllostomids *Carolliinae* and *Stenoderminae*, or the *Megadermatidae*, which feed on large, often sleeping animals, need no such rapid return and so can rely on an energy output which is one hundred to one thousand times less powerful. The "Whispering bats" seem to lie between these two groups.

Leaving *Megaderma*, I introduce *Macroderma*, the largest, as we have learned, and certainly, I do believe, one of the most impressive of all bats. It is with this bat alone, of all the *Megadermatidae*, that I have had personal field experience.

Macroderma is an Australian bat, frequenting the more tropical northern half of the country. Even in Australia the name False Vampire is occasionally used, but the name which I found more common (when the bat was known at all) was Ghost bat. My first (and only) encounter with this bat happened in this way:

I was leading a zoological expedition, for the American Museum of Natural History in New York, into the outback of north central Australia. We had been many weeks in the field and were well "shaken down," that is, our procedures for study and collecting were by then precisely organized and at the highest point of effectiveness we could attain. We had made camps for extended periods in such ecologically varied places as rain forest, so-called open forest, saltbush, plains, river gallery forests, and even a sandbank camp on the barren shores of the Gulf of Carpentaria. We had taken *Pteropus gouldii*, Gould's Flying Fox, *Hipposideros diadema*, the Diadem Horseshoe bat, and other types of *Hipposideros*. We had *Nyctophilus*, the Long-eared bat, and *Chalinolobus*, the Wattled bat; we had shot the Bent-winged *Miniopterus* over a rain forest stream, had taken *Rhinolophus* from a steaming cave in the mulga country, and had captured *Nycticeius*, the Broad-nosed bat, in some tea trees by the Gregory river.

Now we were approaching the Calvert Hills quadrant, past Wallogorang Station in the Northern Territory. The endless miles of black-soil plains were behind us. Ahead lay rocky escarpments and snowy gum trees. Camp was set up at an old copper mine which boasted a clear spring of cool water. Among our first ventures was the investigation of a cave some hundred or so yards above our camp which the aborigines told us was a burial cave. They went on to say that the only inhabitants were their own dead and "Wamurra-murra" and "Wagalla-galla," which their pains-takingly drawn sand pictures told us were bats. We needed no further encouragement but went quickly to the cave.

Upon entering—a "stand-up" entrance—we found it to be a small cave but deep enough to be very dark. At first our lights showed us nothing. Then we found some fresh pieces of bats strewn about—which seemed odd; dead, shriveled, mold-ering bats are not uncommon, but we stopped to comment that this was strange. They seemed to have been torn apart. Suddenly there was a rush of something quite large and seemingly very white past our heads. We turned and snap-fired. Only one small pellet of lead killed a *Macroderma*. We were fortunate, for at such close range we could have blown the bat into pieces. We brought him out into the light—for a quick further search as-sured us there was but the single bat—and all of us marveled at his form and character. The ab-origines who had accompanied us (only to the mouth of the cave) enthusiastically pointed their fingers at the bat and kept repeating "Wagalla-galla, Wagalla-galla."

An hour later, in a state of great rejoicing, we were led to another cave, which was indeed a burial cave where the first was not. It had no stand-up entrance but only a low and narrow fis-sure through which we painfully inched on our backs. It led inwards and upwards past niches filled with the forgotten bones of those aborigines who long ago went to the Land of the Dreaming. Soon the serpentine passage opened up into a sort of vaulted dome with a rock chimney going still further up. We stood up, knees cramped and elbows bruised. Our headlights showed nothing until, in scanning the rock shelves, we experienced another explosive rush of white-bodied bats. In the split second it took to consider how not to shoot one another, the bats were up the chimney and gone. There were five, all *Macroderma*. From far up the impassable chimney we heard muffled shots. One of our party had remained outside and no doubt had seen the exodus. But we were disappointed to find, upon emerging from the cave, that our friend had missed with both barrels.

We spent a full week exploring every cranny and crevice for miles around but we never saw them nor any of their kind again.

On that memorable day we turned to our single specimen, lying dead on a stone, guarded by a black boy. We photographed him, stretched him, measured him, and prepared him with the most tender care. He was indeed a "Ghost bat." No albino—his eyes were black—the bat had pure white membranes, feet, and ears, and a pure white underside. Only his dorsal side showed any color; his back alone was of the palest gray, so pale as to seem almost a dirtied white. The bat is now in the American Museum of Natural History collection.

Later on, in the second cave, we discovered specimens of *Taphozous*, the Emballonuridine Sheath-tailed bat, and deduced, from what remains we could identify, that *Macroderma*'s prey consisted, not of *Taphozous*, but possibly of *Nycticeius* or *Chalinolobus*. *Taphozous*, we found, was the "Wamurra-murra" of the aborigines.

Facing page:
Bat cave

Our relationship with *Macroderma* was short but infinitely sweet, for what naturalist will not glory in a fresh specimen of an exceptionally rare species of animal? As you can see, I can tell you nothing of its habits. *Macroderma*, for all his size and beauty, is no doubt as blood-lusting and careless with his table manners as his cousins. From other reports *Macroderma*, more than any other, is a "cannibal bat," concentrating more on ravaging his kind than on kidnaping birds from their nests. From what I saw of this bat in flight (and from what our companion related from outside), they are extremely swift fliers. I should not be surprised to learn that they are able to pursue and capture their prey in the air, after the fashion of the goshawk.

The only link between our *Macroderma* and the two remaining cannibals is a common appetite. The South American family *Phyllostomatidae* gives us both *Vampyrum*, the largest bat in the New World (wingspread thirty inches) and its near relative *Phyllostomus*. Although I have been to Central America I have seen neither in the field. *Phyllostomus*, however, I have seen in captivity.

That which appealed to me most in the single opportunity in which I observed *Phyllostomus* was that the bat appeared to be from another world. Of course he is; from the New rather than the Old World. But in America I have known many bats, mostly *Vespertilionidae*, of course, but still, they too seemed a world apart from the Spear-nosed bat. I was struck most by his demeanor: he did not look "as a bat should." He had a low, mean air, and about the finest case of nerves I have seen in any animal. His very actions were different: a sort of ratlike scurry, with fre-

Vampyrum, the Giant Spear-nosed bat of Tropical America

quent sidewise motions. Altogether he was not attractive.

My impression is undoubtedly unfair. I know nothing other than that which I have read about neotropical species. But I include it as of interest.

Both *Vampyrum* and *Phyllostomus hastatus* are known to take other bats as well as mice and birds. It could be presumed that their diet parallels that of the *Megadermatidae* and also includes frogs, and, possibly, lizards of some kind. In captivity it has been recorded that in eating a mouse, the prey is carried to the top of the cage, seized by the claw on the thumb, and devoured head first, the tail being discarded (Goodwin and Greenhall). *Vampyrum* roosts in silk-cotton and other trees and usually no other bats are found nearby. *Phyllostomus* roosts in caves or in trees or buildings, often in great numbers.

One word about *Lavia*, the African Megaderm which, because of sanguinary interests, we chose to ignore. *Lavia frons* has a distinction rare among bats outside the flying foxes. *Lavia* is often a day-flying bat. A friend of mine who has collected widely in Africa has told me how he col-

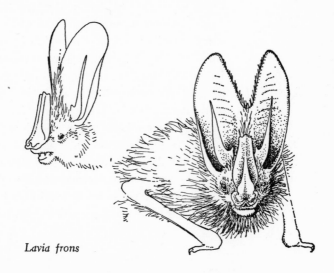

Lavia frons

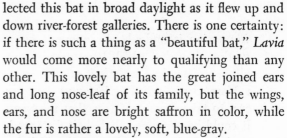

Facing page:
Megaderma,
the Cannibal bat,
attacking a smaller
species

Below:
Macroderma,
carnivorous "Ghost
bat"

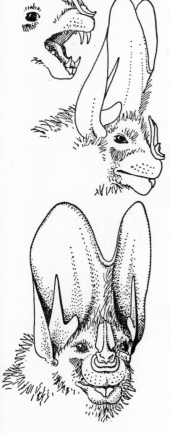

lected this bat in broad daylight as it flew up and
down river-forest galleries. There is one certainty:
if there is such a thing as a "beautiful bat," *Lavia*
would come more nearly to qualifying than any
other. This lovely bat has the great joined ears
and long nose-leaf of its family, but the wings,
ears, and nose are bright saffron in color, while
the fur is rather a lovely, soft, blue-gray.

Quite separate from the carnivores and cannibalistic forms we have just discussed are those
equally odd specialists of the bat world, that I
call, lumping them together, the Fishermen. In
another chapter we have already covered the fact
that such bats exist, but their operations are so
remarkable I think they deserve some further
mention.

There are, purportedly, three species of bats
which catch fish. One large Asian species, *Myotis
rickettia,* is thought to live on fish; their habits
are little known however, and not much more can
be said of them until further work is done. Of
the other two, one, which, also like *Myotis* (and
which, like *M. rickettia,* may well *be* a *Myotis*),
is a Vespertilionid or Simple-nosed bat, *Pizonyx*;
the other is *Noctilio,* of a distinct New World
family, the *Noctilionidae.*

Pizonyx is a striking animal, with a strongly
contrasting dark back and nearly white underside.
It is to be found only along the Gulf of California
in a region unfortunately quite inaccessible for
convenient study. On the isolated island of Pes-
cadora, *Pizonyx* is found to inhabit mainly caves
which are on the shore line just above the tidal
mark, but also, specimens are to be found in small
crannies and under loose stones on the beach.
Their caverns seem to be permeated with the
smell of fish, but it is suspected that their fare is

by no means all from the sea: evidence of beetles and other insects has repeatedly been found.

The wingspread of *Pizonyx* is sixteen inches, and its flight is erratic, after the fashion of many *Vespertilionidae*. Little is known thus far of its actual fishing habits; there is some disagreement about whether this bat gaffs its fishes from the surface with its feet or whether, perhaps, it skims low over the water and catches small fish which jump from the water in frightened efforts to escape the bright reflection of the bat's shining white underparts.

They fly abroad only at night and prefer the most darkened recesses of their caves, for, it has been observed, they seem to sense the diurnal dangers of the thousands of gulls and predatory sea birds which also frequent the same rocky Mexican seacoast. It has been seen to be chased and quickly caught by alert gulls.

Certain attempts have been made to record the sound pulses of *Pizonyx* in captivity but no one has thus far studied this aspect under natural conditions. Dr. Griffin records that the captive animal emitted sound pulses of a type not uncharacteristic of those usually used by other *Vespertilionidae*.

The most dramatic, and best known, of the fish-eating bats is *Noctilio leporinus*. There is another form, *Noctilio albiventer*, which lacks the enlarged hind feet of the former and is known to feed ex-

Pizonyx,
Vespertilionid
Fish-eating bat

clusively on insects. It is almost as if there were two brothers, one of which chose one career and one another. *Noctilio leporinus* has a wide range, from Cuba to northern Argentina; *albiventer* is less commonly distributed. *Noctilio* is physically impressive, being large and extremely muscular and with a wingspread of twenty inches. The fur is very short—almost seallike—and is generally blackish-brown but varies to an ochreous tawny color, and is dramatically highlighted with a very narrow white stripe down the center of the back. The face is oddly framed by extremely pointed ears and there is a much pronounced harelip, which gives it an altogether curious appearance. The flight is powerful and stiff-winged, but not particularly fast.

Noctilio has been the subject of much controversy, for its fishing abilities have been known for over a hundred years. The facts of its actual habits, however, have only recently been revealed, for only within the past few years has the equipment been devised which would disclose its secrets. It is now known that this bat does not catch fish in its mouth in any way but quite literally gaffs them with its very long and substantially clawed feet. Although the animal has been known to fly during the day and even to have flown in company with pelicans, its fishing is generally done at night and all details are lost beyond range of normal sight or hearing.

The reason for the controversy I mentioned was that since nothing could be proved about the bats' actual fishing habits, rumor and loosely-knit hypotheses were, of course, free to race without check. Everyone thought he knew exactly how this fishing was accomplished but it remained for someone to produce graphic proof. There were two principal studies which helped disclose the secrets of *Noctilio*. The earlier, Bloedel's time-sequence photographs, includes some of the most remarkable bat pictures ever taken and Dr. Griffin's work on echolocation has indicated that even more startling information may still be lying hidden. Some splendid motion pictures have been taken which enable the viewer almost to feel as one with the very movements of the animal and which supplement Bloedel's still sequences.

Bloedel's photographs were made with a captive bat enclosed in a screened porch. A shallow pan 30 by 78 inches was filled with water in which small fishes were allowed to swim freely. Cameras and high-speed lighting for their operations were arranged at precise angles to record the bat's every action over the water. What resulted was a magnificent series of pictures which told the entire story. *Noctilio* would fly over the pan, then, skimming very low near water level, would suddenly, by using the calcar "strut," lift the interfemoral membrane between its legs as contact was made and lower its hind legs in full flight, causing twin furrows on the surface of the water. The fish were gaffed by the sharp and highly curved claws as one might gaff a tuna brought to boatside. Then, it was seen that the bat lifted its feet and immediately grasped the fish in its teeth as well as still keeping hold with one or both feet. Finally,

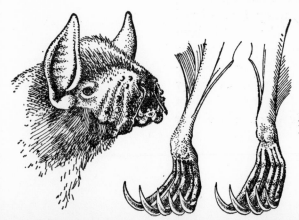

Noctilio,
Fish-eating bat

still in full flight, the bat would grasp the fish more securely in the teeth and fly to the roosting site and eat it. It was seen that fishes lying as much as a full inch under water could be taken— fishes as long as four inches. It was noted, however, that many passes were sometimes taken in order to catch a fish, thus opening the question as to whether it is a random process or one involving echolocation.

At this juncture Dr. Griffin and his exhaustive studies with sound in bats was able to carry the story further. Dr. Griffin, having spent many hours on the rivers of Panama in dugout canoes filled with electronic equipment, was able to say that fishing is selective, the bat lowering its feet at certain times and not others, and that its sonic pulses are not all of one type, but seem to vary, not only in frequency but in amplitude, indicating, possibly, that different types of locatory information are relayed to the bat. The sound frequency was seen to be exceptionally high, which might indicate that, although it would seem unlikely, a fish under the shield of a totally flat film of water might be detected by echolocation. One might expect that as faint ripples were made by a fish near the surface an extremely high frequency of

Noctilio,
Fish-eating bat

sound might be made to guide the bat. Dr. Griffin is cautious to suggest, but does not leave out the possibility, that even if small fish made no ripples whatever, their presence might possibly be detected through the release of small bubbles of air or other gases from their swim bladders.

Certainly all of the puzzles about *Noctilio* are not solved, but the fact is that he is a fisherman—whatever the final secret of his method—and an effective fisherman. Greenhall, in Trinidad, records two further points of interest: as *Noctilio* flew over the water, a distinct swishing sound could be heard. Also, as one bat collided with a flat stone skimmed over the surface, it fell into the water, was seen to swim strongly with its folded wings, then launch itself again into the air, well proving it to be at home in what would ordinarily be considered an entirely alien element.

I remember, not long ago, being asked to explain some of the riddles of bats to my young daughter. She was soon heard to exclaim, "But they get worse and *worse!*" One of the boys, overhearing her remark, retorted, "They don't get worse, just different." And I think he was right.

11

Vampire!

Blood has a texture and odor peculiar to itself.
I do not like it; I mean the heaviness of it in
the air, the glutinous grossness of it. It is not like
water loosed from a dam, but like the dead dis-
interred. It is out of place. Not that it has death
about it; blood has life about it. But of all things,
one thinks of blood (particularly one's own) as
being best where it properly belongs. There has
always been considerable variance of opinion as to
where blood does properly belong. History is one
long and dull tale of bloodletting, and far past
history into mythology and fable, blood, one way
or another, on the outside of wherever it may
have belonged, has been the final argument beyond all others.

One might suspect it would not be the jolly,
sun-loving Italian but the dour, ghost-ridden Slav
who first conjured up the vampire. Of course, the
source of the myth is lost in antiquity, but our
English word, so the dictionary relates, is "Fr., fr.
G. *vampir*, fr. Slavic," all of which is relatively
unimportant but would seem to point somewhat
in the right direction. I rather think it wearing,
myself—all this business about the dead jumping

up out of their graves and wandering about at night sucking blood from persons asleep. But that, in some hundreds of versions and aberrations, is always the way it turns out. Heaven only knows the idea is chilling enough, but it is the dreadful monotony of the tale which bothers me. Poor, dear, old vampire, not to have a good green salad once in a while! I do think, however, that the fellow who finally turned up on the scene and talked of driving a stake of holly through its heart showed a fair turn of imagination.

In very truth, however, it would seem that, as with snails or tripe, it is all in how it is turned out. We have at home a rather large silver platter into which there has been formed a sort of tree-like tributorial channel which terminates, at one end, in a spoon-sized basin. When there is a roast there forms a lovely aromatic pool in this depression. My wife calls this "gravy," though it is not. I love it barring nothing else but oysters perhaps, or *pâté*. I understand, however, that abbatoirs and undertakers have the same sort of efficient arrangement, often in marble. It is, then, I do think, all a matter of viewpoint, time, and circumstance. The African Masai are known to keep cattle and to periodically bleed them through the neck. This hot blood they mix with milk and keep the mixture in skin bags. They are said to eat little else. I think it must be true as I have known some excessively unimaginative people return to say that it is so. There are blood sausages and blood puddings, as we all know; both are to be found in many of our markets. Many races of people are known to utilize blood as a food, and drying blood is a primitive means of food preservation.

Blood, in itself, is a tissue. It is formed of loose cells and plasma, a fluid in which loose cells are suspended. Left on its own, blood is a most healthy fluid, but it can be easily contaminated. If the plastic shell of the skin is broken and an entrance made into the channel systems at a point of large dimension in the tubing (arteries), blood flows out at a rate too fast to regenerate, the ratio of production lowers, and, according to the rate of flow, the body dies. A second possibility is that if the perimetric circulating streams (veins and capillaries) are broken, foreign elements such as germs can enter, circulate, and in much the same manner of reduction, eventually kill the body by offsetting the rational balance of productive regeneration.

And so enters the bat.

Not, Heaven forbid! to imply that bats are really very important in all this as a general thing. Anything which breaks the skin, from a soup tin to a lion's claw, introduces the same possibilities, in greater or lesser degree, of septicity. It is obvious that a rusted and jagged tin left lying in sewage is a far greater hazard than a surgeon's scalpel. However, even the surgeon's scalpel, so recently sterilized, is not always as free as one might think from contamination. The incisive teeth of a specialized bat are as skillfully employed as any surgeon's knife, but they too must be evaluated in terms of the circumstances which lead to contamination, and in no other. No incisive measure is totally safe, but some are exceedingly more safe than others.

Very often we find that one thing or another is named after an animal. In this case, the animal was named after nothing more concrete than a myth. Because an animal was discovered which was found to "suck" blood, and as often as not to take blood from the neck, there was no alternative; it must needs be called *Vampire*. That was that. I should certainly have called it vampire myself, and I think you will agree that you would too.

Scientifically, this bat's name is any of three: *Desmodus, Diphylla,* or *Diaemus.* I will join you in thinking it sounds more like a Greek play in which three villians are introduced to engage forces in some shocking deed. And perhaps— though I doubt it—the scientists who named them may have had a sense of humor. They are all of the zoological family *Desmodontidae,* allied to the Leaf-nosed *Phyllostomatidae,* and all live together in neotropical America. They exist in no other place in the world, nor does any other bat resemble them. The three differ only slightly in but minor points of physiognomy. *Desmodus* is by far the most common and well-known, but their habits are essentially the same.

We spoke a while back of *Vampyrum spectrum.* And while with the *Megadermatidae* we talked (this time in English) of "False Vampires," now, when we come to the true and proper Vampire, we speak in Greek and mumble something about *Desmodus.* Let us now set this straight once and for all. It is indeed *Desmodus* who is the true "Vampire," no other. And I am not being facetious when I say he looks like the very devil. He does.

It does not take much imagination to sketch in some sulphurous wings and an arrow-tipped tail —or however it is the devil is portrayed. He looks the part, he is named for the part, and he acts his part to the letter, for he drains us of our life's blood. Now you have heard me, as we have gone along here together talking of outlandish things, speak in such a way as to represent a sort of apologist for all of batdom. It may seem that way, but, if you will forgive me one word of defense (for "apologist" has a nasty air of the fanatic, it would seem), I would like to say that I am representing only facts. People often say that bats are "loathsome," while at the same time they are out-Heroding Herod at the stock market or whining about the lateness of an inheritance. Nor does a bat assume any kind of human trait; can a bat be "kind"? A bat is simply an animal—much higher than that, a mammal. *Desmodus* never heard of Bela Lugosi, Peter Lorre, or Boris Karloff (whose "scientific" name, I understand, is Bill Pratt!). No one must drive a stake of holly through his heart; he simply dies, like any other bat, and drops to the bottom of his cave to rot, no more nor less than we will rot ourselves. He is a mammal, a bat. This is what he consists of in detail.

Desmodus is a medium-sized and close-furred bat with small pointed ears and a quite small nose-leaf. The wingspread is about fifteen inches. He has a greatly elongated thumb and two soft pads at his wrist—both thumb and pads being tools of his trade, as clamp and glove belong to a surgeon. The calcar, that "spreader" or "strut" at the ankle, which serves to stabilize the interfemoral membrane, is in *Desmodus* but a wartlike knob (how different from the fisherman *Noctilio*, with his need of pedal manipulation!). There is no external tail and the lower lip is deeply grooved. The color is drab gray-brown with lighter underparts. The skull is very broad and the rostrum is greatly reduced, thus affording room for the enormous incisors and canine teeth. The incisor teeth are among the most remarkable in any mammal, being used for but one purpose only, to excise—there is no action whatever of grinding or crushing. The incisors (the very front teeth) consist of only two, which are greatly enlarged, curved, and extremely sharp; the canines (those so obvious in a dog) are also very large, robust, and pointed; the molars or cheek teeth are so small as to be useless, while the lower teeth are also small, and the reduced lower incisors are acutely bilobed. The female bats are larger than the males, the females weighing, on an average, 34 grams and the males from 25 to 28 grams.

Desmodus is more restricted in range than others of the *Phyllostomatidae*, being confined to only the warmer parts of the neotropical belt. It lives in darkened caves and is often found roosting in the same caves which shelter many other kinds of bats—on which, oddly enough, it does not prey. They would appear to breed all year round and have, as do most bats, only one young at birth.

The habits of this bat are truly unique because, as we have said, no other bat—nor any other animal—possesses like tools. *Desmodus'* principal tools are his teeth, but he has other helpful assets as well; his soft pads, long thumb, and cleft lips, and his uncanny ability to hover and alight on one's exposed skin with no more than a zephyr's caress.

This bat, with those extraordinary teeth, takes the merest slice of skin, so that the blood wells up swiftly and surely for his purpose. Is it not astonishing that the animal can so surely, so expertly, accomplish this fact! One need only watch a putter on a golf green or talk to a surgeon to realize that human measurement is not so arithmetically perfect as to have us go about with any overabundance of superiority. Give him his due. You

must. The Vampire bat is as truly remarkable as
any animal that has walked—or flown—the earth.

At just about this time, when the defense is beginning to feel some sort of confidence—when
there is a lull in the air, a few ladies begin to titter,
and the judge shifts from one side of his chair to
the other—at this time, someone will ask the one
electrically charged question: "What about rabies?"

Now there is no lull, no air of confidence, but
a purposeful, very rapid, reshuffling and reassess-
ment. The defense begins anew.

"Well, you are quite right. You could not be
more right. There is indeed rabies to consider."
Then, if he has any sense, he will ask for a recess.

Rabies is a disease of the nervous system in
which violent convulsions and paralysis follow any
attempt to swallow water, hence its other name,
"hydrophobia." Fatal to man and most other
mammals, it is a viral disease, long thought to be
transmitted only by direct contact by bite or
scratch from an infected victim. It is perhaps a
few things more than these, but that is enough.

The disease called rabies (from the Latin
rabidus, "raving," as in madness) is more commonly found in carnivores, perhaps because such
victims as rabbits or mice do not commonly go
about biting other animals. As far as I know, all
mammals are susceptible. Bats have undoubtedly
been spreaders (I believe the term "carriers" is
reserved for those which carry but do not contract
the disease, but I am not certain) of rabies from
the first instance of a bat's having contracted the
disease, or, at least, from the first chain of cir-

cumstance wherein a bat, not a carnivore, was involved. Such an incident was, as likely as not, of ancient occurrence. The newspapers are currently howling about bats spreading the disease. I have two recent articles before me. But surely bats have always been with us. There have always been cyclic fluctuations. It is simply that news travels faster, and even, perhaps—just possibly—at the times of printing, other news was hard to find. Certainly there is an evident interest in the problem these days. As well there should be. I do not think, however, that the spread of rabies through bats is any greater for our having discovered it or for our having an interest.

What is important is that something is being done about it. More and more is being learned about bats. Recently researchers such as Dr. D. Constantine have discovered evidence that rabies is transmitted not only by mouth, but also through nasal and respiratory passages by inhalation of diffused urine—such as might be breathed in within the confines of a cave in which great numbers of bats, including the sick, urinated and defecated in the air. Also, publicity is just beginning to reach a stage beyond sensationalism (as though, having been crying "Wolf!", they are suddenly aware of something actually being at the door), this may have a deterrent reaction on carelessness in the handling of all animals. I doubt that the vigilante approach of wiping out whole populations of bats is a sensible solution; however, in regions where incidence is known and assayed, perhaps no other remedy would have as immediate an effect. It is my personal viewpoint that the most effective combative force for the deterrence of rabies as far as bats are concerned is the transposition of the animal from myth

Desmodus,
True Vampire bat

to fact—which is the singular purpose of this book.

I would like to state now as forcefully as possible, that rabies is indeed a factor to which one must give earnest consideration. I have spoken, since we began, of handling bats—even, in the case of *Desmodus*—of being put in the position of being bitten by bats. My demonstrative suggestions have been, of course, hypothetical. No one, without sound and preconsidered reason, goes about being bitten by anything, bat, dog, or insect. Even outside the realm of pathology there lies the still mainly unfathomed field of allergic reaction, not to mention simple septicity. The blood of which we have spoken is, as we have mentioned, a fine, healthy, and really quite sturdy tissue—as long as it is let alone.

Returning to the Vampire, it must now be clear that the *Desmodontidae* are not the only bats which could and do spread rabies. The Vampire, however, is indeed to be reckoned with because its habits cause it to rupture the skin casing of other animals. And it is a point of singular interest —but about which little is known—that this bat is among the few animals to which rabies is not necessarily fatal. Man is not singled out for attack: cattle, dogs, poultry, and birds are used as fountains of food. And rabies is only one disease transmitted by Vampires. Another is "murrina," a blood parasite most destructive to cattle and horses. Possibly yellow fever may be carried as well as manifold issues of a septic origin. Another distinctly black mark is the rather loathsome result that the open wounds caused by Vampires often, particularly in animals, become infested with fly maggots. There is, of course, an antirabies vaccine as well as like remedies for other diseases. However, it should be clearly evident that prevention is a far better antidote than any other.

Desmodus can be kept in captivity for quite long periods if fed on defibrinated cattle blood. *Diaemus,* however, seems to prefer the blood of birds and goats and will not live on cattle blood. The usual consumption per night is nearly a full ounce. This may be taken from a single animal such as a cow, or from a number of smaller animals. It has been found that a single Vampire will consume about five and three-quarters gallons of blood in a year. If a single cave holds, say, a thousand bats, it means that 5,750 gallons of blood would be needed in a year, or over 15 gallons each night! And all of this from a restricted surrounding territory!

After the wound is made, the tongue is used, not to lap as would a dog, but to form a sort of tube in conjunction with the deep groove in the lower lip, thus channeling the blood in an even flow, as through a straw. The tongue remains protruded and is moved only in pistonlike short strokes. The blood is drawn in *beneath* the tongue, while the top remains free of blood. As the flow lessens, the tip of the tongue is used gently to agi-

Desmodus,
the Vampire bat

tate and thus stimulate the welling fount. Another most interesting part of the physiognomy of *Desmodus* is that where other bats have stomachs of varying size and capacities, so specialized is the Vampire that he would seem by comparison to have virtually no "stomach" at all. Of course he has a stomach, but (when empty) it is extraordinarily tubelike.

Victims are bitten on exposed areas such as the lips, ears, or anal region or on thinly covered areas such as, in cattle, on the neck or horn-bases. Pigs are said to be bitten principally on the nose and, in the case of sows, on the teats, where the nipples may become so scarred as to stop the flow of milk. Small birds are known to have been drained of blood, and thus killed, in a single night. Dogs and carnivores are mostly bitten on the nose or ears, while humans are commonly bitten on the fingers, toes, ears, forehead, or on the lips.

There is yet another facet occasionally brought up which credits the Vampire with exuding a soporific scent which he wafts toward his intended victim by gently hovering in front of its face. Certainly bats have scent glands, but I am very disinclined to believe that any would be capable of putting one to sleep. Quite the other way round, in fact!

Altogether, it would seem that the Vampire is as unsavory as any beast one might imagine. I can think of worse, however. The hyena is one. Another is the human degenerate. But it must be considered that each (except the last) has his purpose, however hidden it may be from us. I caution you not to judge too hastily. The Vampire is scarcely more guilty than your romping kitten: one, the bat, was made to excise and drink; the other, to rend and tear.

V

Goodwin and Greenhall amusingly relate that in Trinidad, when natives are asked about wounds that were obviously caused by Vampires, they often profess to have been bitten instead by a *"soucouyant"* or "jumbie," a blood-sucking evil spirit. The jumbie, they say, is really an old woman who at night sheds her skin and flies off as a ball of fire. She takes her meal on you as does the "vampire," sucking your blood. They say there are ways, however, to trap the jumbie. One is to locate her shed skin and sprinkle hot pepper on it, thus burning her up. Another is to scatter rice outside the door, which she must count, grain by grain, before she can enter and reclaim her skin. If the jumbie is ever caught without her skin she may be disposed of by "placing her in a nail-spiked barrel full of tar and rolling the barrel into the ocean."

I wonder if any bat or any creature, or any thing, is as weird as the human mind?

I hope you will look with charity on *Desmodus*. I cannot, in truth, commend him. He is not of my kind. For me, I can well leave alone quantities of blood and bloodletting. I can do without ghoulies and ghosties, bumps in the night, *soucouyants*, jumbies, murder tales, and vampires. I do not think myself particularly squeamish at all. I simply run toward other things—the light of day and

> *The friendly cow all red and white,*
> *I love with all my heart:*
> *She gives me cream with all her might,*
> *To eat with apple-tart . . .*
> *And blown by all the winds that pass*
> *And wet with all the showers,*
> *She walks among the meadow grass*
> *And eats the meadow flowers.*
> *—*ROBERT LOUIS STEVENSON

12

The Better
to Bite You . . .

There is a sign in Taronga Park, Australia's
largest and one of the world's best zoos, which
reads simply: THESE PARROTS BITE. Nowhere have
I read a message that reaches more incisively to
the heart of a matter. Parrots are not our concern
here, but the remembrance of the simplicity and
naked truth of that parrot sign pitchforks me
heels over head into our next subject concerning
bats with as abrupt an entrance as any I might
contrive. Our subject here is teeth, and we are as-
sured by unassailable affidavits, from the local
postman to Little Red Ridinghood, that teeth, if
they do nothing else, do indeed bite.

But teeth do many other things besides. Not
only do they grasp, or "bite"; teeth can slash, tear,
incise, excise, or gnaw (which is something like
sawing); they can puncture, abrade, or bruise;
they can twist and lacerate; or, finally, they can
crush, grind, and pulverize. Not all teeth do all
things simultaneously, of course, and their diver-
sification is widely distributed. However, as a gen-

eral thing, teeth are inordinately complex, and, especially among the bats, they reach an extreme of modification and complexity.

The Beginning, in the matter of teeth, is *tooth*. The Latin, in this case, gives us no help at all: *dens*, tooth, is simply that. The Greek offers little better: it is still tooth. A tooth is "hard" only as opposed to "soft." The mammalian body itself is but two things, hard and soft parts; that is, components which readily disintegrate at life's cessation, and parts which are more hardy in their make-up. All parts, however, of whatever nature, are living tissue, or tissue once alive—a woven tapestry of cells composed of atomic aggregates. *Os*, the living bone, however hard, is subject to decay —as anyone knows who has suffered the purgatory of the dentist's anteroom. Even the "dead" bone, since it was once a living thing, is subject to eventual decay. Any long survival is mere happenstance, as, for instance, in fossilization.

Of all bone, the tooth is the hardest exteriorly. Its interior, however, is as soft as the most gelatinous tissue. Its composition—of enamel (a spurlike cap, harder than the rest), dentine (foolishly meaning only a "toothlike" amalgam), pulp (equally nondescript, meaning "soft"), cement (a sort of adhesive amalgamate), and a network of nerve endings which radiate through the pulp —tells us nothing whatever except that, as an entity itself, it differs from yet another kind of bone. What "tooth" really means is that it is a spur or protuberance, either at the entrance of or within an orifice, which, when prompted by the trigger of the brain or a cellular structure which acts as a "brain," clamps down (as the "teeth" close in a Venus's flytrap), on a foreign object, i.e., bites. Parrots, dogs, fish, plants, and a small army

of lesser animate things all bite. (Even sucking is a form of biting, for the constrictive labial protuberances would still be a form of "tooth" in that, however gently, they grasp.) It is not until one reaches the lowest of forms, as with certain amoeboid animals or plants, that the bite and tooth give way to absorption.

Turning it all about then: at one end we have the quality of plastic absorption, in which one cannot discern who bites whom with what, if indeed there is any bite at all. At the other end, that with which we are all familiar, the tooth as we know it: a glistening awl or grinding stone, smooth-sided or intricately crenulated, infinitely sharp or the essence of rounded bluntness; an object (quoting from someone we all know) "the better to bite you with, my dear."

The point of all this talk is that teeth are the single most significant factor in the taxonomic separation of any one vertebrate from another, and in the bats they are the one key which brings order out of chaos. Most vertebrates, and nearly all mammals, have teeth of some kind, and the most simple form of tooth is the single cone. It would be a simple thing, one would think, to be able to compare one cone with another. But is it so simple? Such a tooth can be either sharply pointed or blunt, narrow or wide, straight or curved, round, elongated, or multiangular. Even so simple a tooth gives rise to more combinations than one might believe, if the problem is to define and compile each combination for comparison. Consider how gravely insecure one might feel if faced with the problem of comparing the multiconed, multiangular, and multivalleyed surface of a tooth such as this I illustrate—and this in so unsophisticated and everyday a thing as the molar of a cow!

The significance of teeth began to emerge principally in 1883 with Professor Edward D. Cope's "Tritubercular Theory": in essence, that from the most primitive single-coned tooth, two lateral "denticles" arose, and from this basic three-coned ancestor sprang all other forms of teeth. There emerged a comparatively simple indexing by precedence. If a singe cone thus appeared to have denticle piled on denticle to make of the tooth surface a labyrinth of ups and downs, taxonomists quietly sorted out one from the other by a system so arranged as to be transferable to any other tooth of any other animal. Names were given to each cusp and to each valley on the tooth's surface; thus the top of a tooth was seen to have a topography much like a relief map, and could be arithmetically measured and compared.

Of course the passage of time saw Cope's theory rebutted. There arose a "Quadritubercular" theory, the "Embryological," "Premolar-Analogy," and "Polybuny" theories, and others. But generally Cope's theory has found acceptance.

Certain animals have but one tooth—this usually being a throw-back as a result of supraspecialization—but most have many more than one, and these are arranged in various series according to the job they do. This arrangement of teeth is called *dentition*. The teeth themselves, that is, the kinds of teeth, number only four. These vary from the (1) nipping-off type called incisors; (2) the puncturing variety called canines; (3) the chopping and shearing kind called premolars; to, finally, (4) the crushing and grinding sort, called molars. These are arranged according to the use most necessary in maintaining the life of the particular animal. Thus the ungulates, or hoofed animals, having little use for slashing canines, have virtually no canines and instead have great and complex millstones of molars, while the carnivorous dogs and cats possess stilettolike canine fangs and sharp-edged tearing premolars in greater abundance. The arrangements of teeth differ widely between families of animals, and their evolutionary advancement, one from the other, is a fascinating story of interrelationships and preeminence.

The teeth of bats, as we have indicated in a preceding chapter, appear to be closer to those of the insectivores than to any other group. As we have also learned, the habits and make-up of bats seem to parallel nearly every kind of animal but the strictly herbivorous, grazing variety—and even, to resemble those, we have flower-eaters and frugivorous bats. We have seen how our highly specialized types such as the blood-drinking *Desmodus* and the fruit-eating *Pteropus*, have one his incisive tooth, and the other his prying awl. And we have discussed how the teeth of the earliest known bats seemed, with but one exception, to resemble those of the insect-eaters of today.

Bat's teeth show wide variation not only between families but between each of the major genera. Indeed, it is often this single differentiation which separates one genus from another. The greatest number of teeth known among bats is thirty-eight, whereas in the insectivores the greatest number is forty-four. No conclusion is to be reached from these numbers, however, for there exists considerable variation in both groups. The four major groups of teeth—incisors, canines, premolars, and molars—are found in bats as they are in most mammals, but also as it is with the others,

hooked, milk teeth

Eptesicus

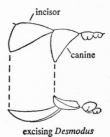

incisor

canine

excising *Desmodus*

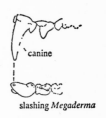

canine

slashing *Megaderma*

premolar

chopping *Eptesicus*

Kinds of teeth   grinding *Epomophorus*

molar

molar

crushing *Artibeus*

bats seem to drop one or the other of the tooth types, depending on their mode of living.

The process of specialization in bats, it would seem, has reduced the teeth rather than caused them to gain in numbers. The insect-eaters—presupposed to be the earliest types—have many sharp-bladed premolars and molars connected by equally sharp, knife-edged crests, which act as multiple "choppers" quickly to reduce the often hard-shelled fragments of their prey. The fruit bats have a far different need: after having pierced and torn apart husks, they must have the equipment as well to crush and grind; they have evolved much wider, flat-topped molars for this purpose. The variance and substitution in evidence when one compares the entire generic structure of bat teeth formulae is amazing. Certain genera lose one of a possible three teeth from one group while others will lose more, gain more, substitute or add, to one's utter consternation. The one soothing consolation to be found is that one discerns a very great level-headedness employed in this tool-usage; as though the dispensing Steward was indeed well-versed in his trade.

"Our own bats," that is, North American bats, are all insect-eaters. Their formulae run a full mouthful, from the maximum 38, through 36, 34, 32; *Eptesicus*, 30, to *Eumops*, 28. Most of the world's Vespertilionids follow much the same pattern. The Old World *Hipposideridae*, still insect-eaters, average 30.

The long-fanged, cannibalistic *Megaderma* tells us plainly, by his lack of incisors, that slashing is his business. *Epomophorus*, one of the African fruit bats, by the general paucity of all teeth, and in particular of the molar teeth, shows us that the fruit or flowers and nectar upon which he feeds is generally soft in nature. The skull also gives two additional clues in that the canines are weak and the molars much flattened and not intricately grooved. By way of contrast, the American fruit bats *Brachyphylla* and *Artibeus* have extremely wide, deeply crenulated grinding molars and sharpened, heavily based canines—tools of one whose fruit husks and pulp are of a sturdier kind.

Our old friend *Desmodus*, whose surgeon's scalpels are overgrown and greatly sharpened incisors, has no need for either chewing or grinding; it has the premolars and molars reduced to little more than minute knobs, both together being smaller than the canine alveolus, or tooth socket.

One thing remaining which we have not mentioned, and one which further complicates matters, is wear. Teeth are growing tissues, and wear is inevitable. Certain of the rodents have an ever-sharpening, self-perpetuating arrangement by which wear only improves functioning. Bat's teeth, like our own, wear down, and, eventually, wear out. The milk teeth (often interestingly hooked on the ends so that they cling more readily to the mother's fur) are short-lived and fall out to be replaced by adult teeth. The adult teeth show progressive stages of wear and are often confusing in the advanced stages by their seeming departure from the tritubercular plan, which indeed seems to persist throughout all mammals. Bat's teeth do not, however, ever seem to wear out to the degree of nonfunctioning; the bat's life span is conveniently regulated so that, like the one-horse shay, both fade out together.

Chilonatalus

Vampyrus

Desmodus

Promops

Skull variations

Leptonycteris

Centurio

Mormoops

The teeth are the most important taxonomic criterion, but of course the other "hard parts" are all important as well, particularly the skull. The bat's skeletal structure, in its many and varied types, is far too elaborate a framework to discuss in any detail here. In general, it resembles man's own skeletal make-up, except, of course, for the elongated fingers and the knee joints, which bend in a way opposite to man's—as the sketch will show. Each measurement of each single bone is taken into account, as are the curvatures, protuberances, and angles of any point on its surface. For instance, the knobs and obtuse curvatures of a single bone are given many names. This may all seem too fussy for your palate, but I can assure you that even such detailed annotations are often not enough when comparisons are being sought. Scientists are bound by no Hippocratic oath, but they must be as assiduous and unrelenting in their quest among inanimate parts as any medical doctor performing on living tissue.

The skull itself is even more complicated a hieroglyphic than the rest of the skeleton. The skull is a box, as it were, formed of jigsaw parts and molded into unbelievable varieties of conformation. This box holds all of the nerve ends, all of the delicately balanced sensory organs, the principal orifices of entrance into the body, as well as that gelatinous, gray computer called the brain. The box is chambered and supported; has holes drilled through it to direct nerve cables; it has inner platforms, bridges, filters, shell-like covers, sockets, joints, cavities, and stanchions . . . all these, and more, in a bat's skull only half an inch long! There is a different skull for each species—which, you will remember, brings us to over two thousand. Each of these differs one from the other in values so extreme as to seem to defy analysis. Some few extremes of conformation are pictured, but only by way of curiosity—successfully to attempt any comparative study would take not one, but a hundred books, if any degree of accuracy and meaning were to be achieved. It is not, then, a pusillanimous reaction which prompts me to suggest that we bypass any further details in skull structure. As with passing by a lion's cage, it is best remembered that skulls hold teeth—and teeth are one of the best lessons devised by Nature in instructing us that valor should be tempered by wisdom.

13

Maternity
Ward

Bats, being mammals, are born like everyone else. Thus, in one sentence, might one begin and end this chapter.

It is quite as simple as that. Were we discussing the Monotremes, or egg-laying mammals—still bona-fide mammals, as the books go—we might well have new horizons to scan. Whales might pose a question or two along the way. But there is nothing really new or startling about the reproductive cycle in bats. Then why do we go on? Because there is nothing left to do. I mean that we cannot make of it anything else. Neither we nor bats lay eggs or subdivide or have exploding seed pods. Bats fly, and we mix colors and spread them around and give them names, and we build things —but when it comes to birthing we both sit right down without much nonsense and give birth. It would all seem very simple indeed. Bats are thus born: I cannot escape talking of it.

But I will tell you that I stand in awe of birth.

164

I know, of course, the usual textbook details, and so do you. I have watched children of my own spring into life—but for all I knew they might have been spawned from the sea. As with flour tins, hairpins, costume jewelry, and untidy closets full of other female impedimenta, birth and its meaning are part of an inner world forever denied to males. I feel rather as one who accidentally fell through a skylight into a maternity ward.

For my own part, I feel ancient. I cannot remember my mother's womb, nor any chill when I was torn from it, nor my mother's breast. But I am a mammal; I know that I must have experienced it all. I have tried to recapture some dim understanding as my own children have been born. They lay, I remember, like legs of lamb, or else howled their heads off—and I made a fool of myself scratching at them through a window glass. I have paused silently to ask the dead to cast back some sort of sign. They lay like my just-born child; not caring. Maturity would seem to be a high noon between the freshet-rush of childhood and the embers of senility. I find there is a glare through which I cannot see. Why I should be sitting here on a hot afternoon in July, with the sun pouring onto my back in soothing ladles, and talking of birth and bats seems quite beyond me. But I do know, really. It is because I have grown to care very much about such things.

Whether one is a bat or a cat, a whale, or a junior congressman from Illinois, the fact that one is a mammal somewhat stereotypes the processes by which things are done. Except for some ill-bred cats and occasionally a rather reprehensible dog, the processes of reproduction generally take on an aura of privacy and retirement. But as I say, the sequence remains unalterably the same. Man would seem to run unchecked, but in her cyclic passage woman is chained to the solemn timbre of the zodiac. Each female, human or bat, runs by the stellar clock which times her species. And each (of course, being women!) has fluctuations and divergencies from the norm. However, the norm for any species sharply restricts the latitudes of variance. In the human female the menstrual cycle lasts about a month. But primates and only primates are definitely known to "menstruate" or have "menstrual cycles." Other mammals, including bats, have "oestrous" cycles in which receptive periods show great variance. In the bat, the period of receptivity is either once, twice, or more, a year; no one really knows. But one thing is known about bats: although their "outsides" differ greatly from ourselves, their "insides"—at least as far as reproduction goes—differ very little. It is in the oestrous cycle that the principal differences are to be found. It is well known that lengths of oestrous cycles are widely variant. Certain of the rodents are exceptionally short-cycled, while certain large ungulates and the *Proboscidae* are very long-cycled. Bats are generally long-cycled, but there appears to be a variation in the time schedules of the ovulatory process. Hibernating species, particularly, pose a problem of deferred and restricted schedules, unknown—or at least unusual—in humans.

Fertilization introduces the male animal and is rigidly defined; it does not include insemination, but only the actual union of sperm and egg. Again, we have a problem of cyclic activity. Certain mammalian species, such as man, regenerate sperm throughout the year, but bats, and other species, are restricted by cyclic breeding seasons. Male bats are constructed exactly as the human male, and both scrotum and penis are remarkably similar. The one exception to this similarity is that, since man's regeneration is constant and the bat's seasonal, the scrotum and penis in bats are seasonably either shriveled or hugely expanded. And it is of extreme interest to note that in certain hibernating bats the process of fertilization has been deferred at a certain stage of its progression. With *Myotis*, *Eptesicus*, *Vespertilio* and *Plecotus* the ejected semen is stored in the uterus; in the Rhinolophids, however, the sperm are stored in an outpocket of the vagina in a viscous matrix. In the human male, semen has a life of but a few hours, but in these bats, at least, there is the unique phenomenon that the arrested semen remains alive during the entire period of winter months. In the spring this mucous matrix, or plug, is passed by the female and the live semen continue their journey toward the egg.

The breeding season of bats differs among the various genera. In the northern hemisphere the genitalia of certain male bats begin to enlarge and copulation takes place in October and November. The female ovum descends in the spring and at that time fertilization begins. In other genera, copulation takes place in the spring. In the southern hemisphere, the same general timing is observed, but reversed, to correspond with the southern seasons. Certain tropical genera are suspected of having more than one breeding season, and captive bats of the genus *Rousettus* have produced young during every month of the year. It is obvious that much is to be learned in this area.

The copulatory act in bats has been studied in certain cave species. No overt revelation has resulted outside the fact that the act is consummated in classic quadrupedal position, belly to back. As far as I am informed, only the human species and certain lizards copulate front to front. Whales, having no other choice, are known to lie side by side, rolling half-over in the water. Certain bats—our own Red bat for one—are alleged to copulate while in the air. Most bats, however, are thought to couple while hanging from a support. The female's interfemoral membrane, if present, is raised over the back by the tail.

I have witnessed the mating process numerous times. In my personal observation there was never an opportunity to detect any semblance of courtship. I strongly doubt the existence of a courtship, or at least one of any distinction, although there is scarcely a female of any species who will not in some way object to a male whose ardor and finesse are either more or less than she anticipates on her own rightful level of values. I have witnessed more than one instance of a female *Myotis* objecting most strenuously, by both kicking and biting; but whether it was indignation or satiety which led to the outbursts, I could not say. The males, at any rate, seemed to lose out in their proposed intentions.

The rate of embryonic development in bats, once the egg has been fertilized, is not constant between species, and very little is known to any degree of exactitude. Generally, the gestation period is considered to be around six months in the large fruit bats and two or three months in the *Microchiroptera*—a long time when one considers that that of a young mouse of the same size is three weeks.

Birth—whether of a nebula from the womb of Eternity or of a bat in the blackness of its cave— is a solemn moment; that single arithmetic progression can never have a duplicate. It is one's own. It comes suddenly, as came the summer shower that rages at my window. It is no surprise to the mother, who has ample warning. The child is always ready. It comes suddenly and it comes irreversibly, snatching us from security and hurling us into the glare and the cold, as one snatched from a winter fire and thrown naked into the snow. No one notices the birth of a bat, but it is born; no one can change the fact.

The young bat emerges breech-first; the feet appear, and, after five minutes, a crumpled handwing. The mother struggles more until the shoulders are free, then the young bat helps itself by pulling with its thumbs against the mother's thighs. The infant is born on his back, without a vestige of hair and attached by a two-inch long umbilical cord.

Except for certain of the *Pteropodidae*, in parturition the mother reverses her upside-down position to hang by her thumbs. She stretches her legs to their fullest extent and curves her tail under, thus spreading her interfemoral membrane to act as a receiving cradle. After the young has fully emerged she licks it clean, holding on with one wing while holding and turning the young bat with the other. Then she resumes her normal position on the branch, bites off the umbilical cord and then sometimes eats the placenta. *Myotis lucifugus* only rarely eats the placenta, *Tadarida* (a Molossid) and *Desmodus* probably never do. The young one is held in position and attaches itself to a teat. The total time for parturition is less than twenty minutes.

It can be construed that bats of vastly different species may vary not only in the place but in the mode of birth. It may be that some species give birth in a semiprone position, as on a rock shelf or in a tree cavity, but this is mere speculation.

Certainly those bats, such as the *Pteropodidae*, which have no tail or interfemoral membrane, and which therefore can make no soft delivery cradle of skin must, as they are known to do, keep the normal position, and may give manual assistance as well as the exit is effected. Some other genera may also give birth while hanging in their normal position, and instances are recorded where considerable labor pains were felt. It is also known that scraping to break open the placental sac is sometimes employed. Breech births appear to be normal except in certain Pteropids.

The number of young in most genera is usually limited to one, although twins do occasionally occur in bats much as the human female is subject to variance. There is one exception among bats in which multiple births appear to be fairly common. The American genus of "red" bats, *Lasiurus borealis*, and its cousin *L. cinereus*, frequently has not only two young but sometimes three or even four, although one is considered to be normal. I know of no comparative exceptions among human races which I can categorically state, although I believe I have heard it mentioned that there is a greater incidence of multiple births within certain bounds of society.

The postnatal care of bats seems to be on a somewhat primitive level. The male bat takes no apparent interest, if, indeed, he is anywhere around at the time. Males of many species appear to live separately or in totally male congregations for much of the year except at the breeding season. It is not known, however, by whose choice this segregation is directed. Monogamy, as such, if it exists at all, would seem to be a rarity among most genera. Cave species, especially, are suspected of multiple interchange, very possibly with a total lack of knowledge surrounding the identity of the inseminating male. The female seems concerned only with the point of satiety, at which point she must assert her dissent. This, though it may appear at first orgiastic, is no more so than a dog bitch separated from a protective male; the season of mating is a season of urgency.

After the young bat is born and is attached to a teat, the mother, upon feeling able to do so, is free to fly off in search of food. The baby is prepared for the rigors of tandem flight by the sharp claws with which it clings to the mother's fur and by its specially designed, hooked milk teeth, which, when not engaged in suckling, are well adapted to assist the claws in holding fast to the fur. Soon, however, as the burden of a growing infant becomes too much to bear in flight, the mother places the young one by itself on a branch or cave shelf while she reconnoiters alone, returning periodically to feed it. The mother nurses her young until it is able to assimilate more solid food. It is not known to me as a fact, but I suspect that, as with birds, the mother first weans the young one mouth to mouth on presoftened food before attempting to give it solids.

When the baby bat is old enough to fly, it first strengthens its wings by beating them from a stationary perch. The mother must make overtures, at least, in the matter of flying lessons. Very little is known about the airborne schooling, but the mother must also teach at least the rudiments of aerial hunting. There are reports that the mother takes the young bat in the air and drops it, after the fashion of a jet bomber carrying a missile or smaller aircraft—but I have never seen it, nor do I know anyone who has. I have seen young bats left by their mothers in some very much exposed places, and reason from this fact that the mother is either careless in her choice or that in each case there was an extraneous urgency beyond my knowledge. I strongly suspect, however, that the latter is not the case and that the mother is simply—since bats are prone to only a minimum of predation—unthinking, and, in being so, a much more primitive being.

It appears, both in caves and in camps, that in falling from either the mother's breast or from a temporary perch, the young bat would be virtually doomed. This would be so not altogether because of the violence of the fall, except in the case of the very young. Apparently, unless the young bat falls only to a lower shelf or branch, the mother is incapable of going to the floor or ground to pick it up. Again, this is not—although it may be diffi- cult—a physical impossibility, but seems to lie in the realm of a mental incapability to cope with a situation beyond the established order of instinc- tive reaction. As with a rat in a "Skinner box" or a pigeon or chicken going through the experi- ments in stimulative reaction, the bat—or at least certain genera—could, I believe, well be taught to reason, but in the wild, under the stress of momentary crisis, it is not reason but instinct

Nursing young

which functions. Interesting observations have been made in this area in that adult bats, having been aroused by the high-pitched cries when a young bat fell and was helpless, have been seen to swoop low, circle about, and even to hover over the hapless youngster, "as terns rally to a wounded companion," but none actually touched or helped it; the adults' concern soon subsided and the young one was left to die (Miller).

However, Allen relates that another observer

verified that when a young bat was brought to him in the daytime and hung in an exposed place in the house, after dark a Pipistrelle bat flew in through a window, suckled the baby, and flew off with it clinging to her breast. Yet another observation (Godman) tells of a young bat having been captured and carried in the hand for some blocks through Philadelphia while the mother followed in the air and finally alighted on the observer, sought her young, and took it to her breast.

These instances surely seem to refute any lack of parental concern and give evidence only of inconclusive examination of the habits and mental processes of bats. I do think that bats are burdened with mental incapacities much as are other species which have reached so high a degree of specialization. One would not expect, for instance, that a dolphin—known to have a high mental level—would be capable of leaving its element and floundering over any considerable portion of dry land to rescue its young. That animal, like the swooping but ineffectual bats, would very probably exhibit much distress, even to the point of coming to the very edge of the water, but would, in the end, be totally unable to effect a rescue.

Bats have not been examined to any great degree for their comparative mental prowess. When they are—and it will be soon, for scientists throughout the world are increasing their efforts in this direction—I cannot foresee any exceptional disclosure, for, as I reiterate, they are beings of extreme specialization and must compensate in some way for the release which elevates them beyond the scope of other species. Still, as we have learned by tracing their physiognomy through the channels of their very bowels, bats are mammals, and as mammals they must live and die. We ourselves fly—higher than bats—and will go higher perhaps than man can dream ... but, like the bats, we too, no more or less, are prisoners of the subtle rhythm of our mortal loins.

14

Points South: Migration

A s I write, there are already garlands of tree
swallows strung on the telephone wires, and
a seeming superabundance of towhees, all scratching up with both feet, as they do, sending up small
explosions of oak leaves and threatening the tender roots of my new rye grass on the path. There
are cars locked bumper to bumper on the great
highway five miles off, all roof-crammed with
stifled humanity trying to squeeze dry the last of
summer, as my wife's jelly bag hangs on its hook
squeezing the season's first grapes, slowly revolv-
ing, draining off drop by drop in a warm aura of
unbelievable pungency and drunken wasps. Soon
there will be geese pounding down through our
estuary and crisp frost edgings on the tidal marsh.
There will be Red bats found hanging in the bay-
berry bushes above the tide. Actually, it is still
high summer, though it is beginning to wane. The
sun is hotter than in July. But everything somehow seems restless. Everyone is moving. Migration
is at hand.

Not that it ever stops, really. Migration is seasonal in that it affects us and the things we have come to know. It is seasonal in that natural things follow natural seasons. But migration is for the migratory. Some things and some people never migrate. I once talked with a very old woman in North Carolina, whose proudest boast, "I have never been out of Mecklenburg County in all my life," aroused the greatest doubts in me until I discovered it was true. Much the same attitude can be found in New Hampshire, Surrey, or New South Wales. On the other hand, we all know people who visibly shudder at the mention of winter. They say, "I'd rather die." And they might. They fly (now quite literally) to Florida or the Côte d'Azur, as surely, and even more swiftly, than does the swallow. Some of us were born, apparently, to feel the pulse of the sea and the sky; others, to stand rooted to the earth with the stoic resistance of an upland stone.

Bats, too, are thus so simply divided into the migratory and nonmigratory. There seems to be no rule which regulates this division; rather, almost, it would appear that they have been chosen as boys for a game, some from here and some from there, helter-skelter and indiscriminate. So firmly do I believe in natural accord, however, I cannot feel that so reckless a process is really in use. There are reasons why some bats migrate, and reasons why some—so outwardly similar—do not.

Migration is not all so simple as fleeing from the cold. Food is often as urgent a problem, and other reasons for movement among bats vary greatly, depending on locale and circumstance. Examples of local migration can be caused by the destruction of natural habitats, monsoon seasons, air pollution, and continued predation, such as by man. But age-old habits are difficult to break, and often whole populations will choose to die rather than alter their established pattern of life. All other migrations, even those pressed by food shortage, are insignificant, however, compared with the rhythmic obedience paid to the change in seasons.

There are few of us left unimpressed by the seasonal migration of the Golden plover and certain allied species of birds. They breed in the far reaches of the arctic tundra, wing south through the north temperate belt, beat through the tropics, burst into summer again in the southern Temperate Zone, and glide on to the bleak shores of Patagonia, as far south as naked land extends. At the next turn of seasons the same birds wheel about, head north, and do it all over again. Many other animal species, even butterflies and dragonflies, undertake trips of spectacular distance, though less extreme than the plover. Whales migrate great distances, and some land animals as well, although with terrestrial species it is food which most appears to motivate movement.

No bat, as far as is known, has anything resembling the range of birds. For one thing, there are relatively few bats of any kind which penetrate to the cold belts of the temperate zones where seasons vary to extremes. In the United States there are fewer species in Massachusetts than are to be found in Georgia, there are fewer in Sweden than in Spain, and far fewer in Melbourne or Santiago than in Brisbane and São Paulo. The tropics, where there are no true seasons, are chock-a-block full at all times, as we know, like chicks round an incubator. The evident purpose of those hardy, nonhibernating species, which do breed in less temperate regions, is not to desert the tropics but only to reach a clime in which survival is possible during the periods of cold.

Only two genera of American tree bats migrate, *Lasionycteris*, the Silver-haired; and *Lasiurus*, the genus which isolates the two seemingly different species, *L. borealis*, the Red bat, and *L. cinereus*, the Hoary bat. Of the three, the Red bat is by far more common and in evidence to the observer. For one thing, his breeding range is of far greater latitude, and his habits of more or less friendly "integration" with humans, that is, swooping or hovering round the homely glow of street lamps, or, often, of flying virtually in daylight, make him seem less a specter of the dark than a "swallow-gone-wrong" (which, in the lopsided logic of humans, is almost "all right").

Of the other two, the Hoary—a candidate surely, for the world's most beautiful bat—is too rarely encountered to be known at all well, and the Silver-haired is a lover of watercourses and ponds, forsaking Main Street and generally shunning houses. The Red and Hoary bats travel as great a range in miles as is known in bats: from the Canadian forests to the borders of Mexico, a distance of at least a thousand miles. They have been observed both in Bermuda and in Hawaii, which is astonishing, but—remembering the caution we are bound to apply—it is also known that these bats, along with birds, often hitchhike aboard ships; thus, resting in the rigging, they could as well appear in Marseilles or Madrid. There have been numbers of reports of bats settling down on ships, mostly coasting vessels, or on vessels inshore. One (Thomas, 1921) reports that a flight of over a hundred bats—from which both Red and Silver-haired were captured—settled on a ship twenty miles off the North Carolina coast. Other reports have been made much further out at sea. It is my own opinion that, on straight flight, on extremely favorable winds, Bermuda could well be a possibility. But knowing the stomach capacity of these bats, their probable speed, something of their stamina, and having bucketed the distance from New York to Hamilton in a sailing yacht, I, personally, doubt that bats really fly very great distances over water and survive. I think that hitchhiking is by far the likelier explanation of records of their appearance on any pelagic island.

But nonetheless the Red and Hoary bats do fly great distances. Bat banding has proved this point beyond question. The Silver-haired, it is suspected, not only flies less in distance (as a general rule), but also, not infrequently, "over-winters," a term similar to, but not synonymous with, hibernation.

No less dramatic is the case of the Mexican Free-tail (*Tadarida brasiliensis mexicana*), another long-distance flier. Marked animals have been recovered as far as nine hundred miles from the banding site. This bat summers in the southwestern United States and winters deep in Mexico.

There is little truly accurate data on the coming or leaving of the migratory bats to their northern breeding grounds; there are only isolated records for individual locations. As are all facets of bat study, migration is today receiving considerable attention. As I write, I have on the table before me the latest data and some specimens, brought only yesterday, from a banding station. The latest techniques employed deserve I think, a more detailed description.

Bat banding began, actually, with Spallanzani in 1794, when that remarkable Italian "marked" bats by blinding them. Even though blinded, you will remember, they did return to their bell tower and were thus recorded as the first "returns." It is a curious fact indeed that the first genuine attempts at banding, outside random experiments, were not made until the 1930s. During that period there began a simultaneous interest in exploring old mines and caves in the northeast United States and in Germany. Such now well-known scientists as Donald R. Griffin, William J. Hamilton, and Charles E. Mohr were instrumental in the first really serious banding of bats. I remember others; keen, rugged, and healthy young men, long since dead in World War II. Under the influence of the infectious enthusiasm and drive of these pioneers, I banded my first bats in 1937.

Most bat banding in the early stages was done with cave bats and such studies as longevity, breeding habits, and local migrations were probed with consummate interest. The banding itself was, and remains, a simply process. As with bird banding, a small and very light aluminum band, numbered in series and with a short plea to "Write F. and W. Service, Wash. D.C. USA"— and a number—is attached to the animal. Various placements were tried: the foot is too small and ill-adapted, so the usual point of attachment is on the forearm. No restriction of movement is encountered; the bat immediately learns to compensate, apparently, for the small weight imbalance. Thousands of these bands have been used and returns are a matter of the initial attachment. As can be well understood, if colonial bats are banded, their habits will virtually guarantee numerous returns (presuming their survival) if one only searches in likely places. In the case of migrating species, of course, one return in many hundreds might be looked upon as remarkable. In discussing hibernation I shall be pressed to speak again of banding, but here, let us return to the migratory species.

Until very recently little has been done with the migratory bats, that is, not the colonial species which engage in "local migrations," or, to use a better term, "mass movements," but the three species of which we have spoken which migrate great distances. At first studies were restricted to sight observations, shooting bats in passage, and capturing occasional live migrants. Then, with crude nets, some experimenters succeeded in banding some tree bats along the coastal flyways. It was C. H. Merriam in 1888 who first gave us evidence that bats also used the "flyways" followed by migratory birds. Such migratory routes follow either some longitudinal barrier, such as coastlines, mountain ranges, or great river systems, or natural wind-flow or weather cycles. It was found that nets could capture migrating bats if placed at strategic geographical points and at proper heights.

Bird banding long preceded work with bats. Netting birds has been an art employed for centuries, and marking birds is not by any means a new procedure. Nor is bird banding for scientific purposes a new thing, but in recent years it has taken on an increased impetus and remarkable results are being obtained on a world-wide scale. Particularly in America has there been a gigantic increase of interest in a short period of time. One of the turning points in increasing interest came with the introduction of so-called "mist nets," first

Bat banding

WRITE F.&W. SERV.
64 - 23849
WASH. D.C. U.S.A.

pioneered by the Japanese. Made of hair-fine silk, they form a gossamer lacework six feet high by thirty feet long. Birds, upon flying into this nearly invisible mesh, become inextricably entangled but come to no harm if removed by an experienced hand. In such a manner are hundreds of thousands of birds captured for banding each year. Seeing such a performance with birds, researchers on bats tried their hand at the same game. There was nothing like the success found with birds. It was discovered that bats, with their sensory guidance system, could nearly always avoid the nets.

My results, when I first tried mist-netting in Australia and New Guinea, were astonishing, for many of the smaller, previously thought rare fruit bats plopped into my nets like missiles. Even many of the large bats were easily caught. I, too, quickly discovered, however, that the "sonar-equipped" insect-eaters were as adept in New Guinea as they had been proved to be in America. My exceptions, however, were gratifying; I found that dense fog often confused these bats, and I made exceptionally good collections on foggy nights.

Migratory bats are still an enigma in that they remain hard to trace. Although they follow the known bird flyways, they not only fly by night but have, as we have said, a device that generally prevents their capture along with night-flying birds. But some become confused, particularly on foggy nights, and are accidentally killed by flying into lighthouses or beacons; others seem to be "jammed" by certain radio waves issuing from transmitters and die by flying into steel girders. But most migratory bats apparently enjoy a blessed immunity from the perilous semiannual gauntlet through which birds must fly.

As with most immunity, however, that which has so long protected the migratory species is beginning to wear thin. A breakthrough has been made. There is no electronic marvel in this case: it is simply that where small-scale mist nets have failed, large-scale netting is showing some results. What has happened is that bat banders are now being assisted by the behemoth of organized bird banders. It is as a result of that cooperation that bat specimens are on my table.

There are numerous bird-banding groups. One of the largest stations, I am told, is in Poland, and England has always been a leader and driving force behind any such purpose. But one of the world's largest bird-banding operations is only forty-five miles from my house. Under the auspices of the Eastern Bird Banding Association, in cooperation with the U.S. Department of the Interior, and various Audubon societies and bird clubs, this station occupies a site on one of the numerous peninsulas along the coast of New Jersey, directly on one of this country's principal migratory flyways. Mrs. Stanley S. Dickerson leads a well-coordinated team of volunteer workers who run the station on a twenty-four-hour-a-day basis during the peak periods of the autumn migration season. The numbers of birds captured, identified, measured, weighed, banded, and released (a process which for an individual bird, can take as little as one minute) has reached the staggering number in a single three-month season of 25,389! Through Mrs. Dickerson's kindness the station staff is alerted to the capture of bats as well as birds, and new patterns of bat behavior are being brought to light.

The reason for this success lies, as I have said, not in a new technique but in a vastly enlarged

use of the old nets. Where under ordinary circumstances one is fortunate in keeping half a dozen
nets in operation, this station each night operates
as many as sixty-five! With this "saturation netting," even though bats are ordinarily able to avoid
them, the odds are so improved that the balance
is in favor of a small but steady number of captures. There are certain to be enormous numbers
which pass unhindered, but this very week no
fewer than eleven Silver-haired bats were taken
during a single night. This is not only the largest
number ever caught at one time but it tells us
something suspected but heretofore unproved:
that *Lasionycteris*, at least, does definitely—at
times—migrate in closely-packed mass flights.
This is further borne out, in this instance, by the
fact that six bats were taken from a single net.
Also, such mass flights seem to be made up of one
or the other sex, usually young males. There are
sight records of Silver-hairs over coastal waters
which *seemed* to be flying in loose groups—but
never any definite evidence. I have shot them
during migration time when I thought there were
rather more numbers in the air than usual. Now
one thing has been unquestionably proved: bats
not only migrate on the same flyways as birds;
they travel *with* the waves of birds. The results
obtained through the cooperation of the E.B.B.A.
may well multiply to such dimensions as to become another important milestone.

At times there are diurnal flights of migratory
bats. There are few positive identifications of
species, but to an experienced observer these bats
are not difficult to separate on the wing in at least
reasonable light. Certainly Red bats have been
seen in diurnal flight; not in "flocks" or closely-
held groups, but in a long flight pattern of single

bats, flying leisurely and straight, in contrast to their erratic hunting sorties. I have seen no such pronounced movement, but on September 16, 1962, there was such a one at the New Jersey banding station, and I have witnessed late afternoon flights of Red bats in which individual bats seemed to fly slowly and straight from horizon to horizon in a southerly direction. Only last March, I remember, on a warm day but at a time when much snow lay deep in the orchard, at precisely two o'clock in the afternoon, I saw an unmistakable Hoary bat which flew overhead in steady flight for seven full minutes (seemingly as migratory hawks are seen to "mill" before setting a direction). Then, with seeming great purpose and unhurried flight, it flew over the estuary and disappeared into the north. I cannot believe that this bat was a cripple or one which over-wintered; I believe it was a migrating bat and, at two o'clock, the sun, though low, was bright and warm.

The same kind of communal use of flyways takes place in Europe—where the Noctule bat, *Nyctalus*, (not unlike our American Hoary bat) is known to fly from Scandinavia to Germany—and undoubtedly between north central and eastern

Machaerhamphus, the Bat Falcon, pursuing *Mops,* African Free-Tailed bat

U.S.S.R. and southern latitudes. It is as yet undetermined whether the Red and Hoary bats of South America migrate northward in reverse season, but it is virtually certain that they do. In Africa and Australia, fruit bats are often seen in migrations, but these are generally thought to be food migrations.

We have mentioned that bats, in general, would seem to have something of a rare gift in not having many natural enemies. Bats do have enemies, of course, but it is obvious that whoever might have a taste for them would have to be extraordinarily spry, at very least.

Our own bats probably have as few enemies as any other animal group. Naturally, any predator-type animal will eat bats if the opportunity arises. The Virginia opossum, notorious for having a cast-iron palate, will occasionally come upon tree bats. In like manner, so will the skunk, fossicking about in the bowels of a windfallen tree. House cats, of course, will pursue them with relish, and the weasel tribe, perhaps most of all, will dine on bat meat. But to any terrestrial animal, bats are a delicacy only accidentally come by. The principal enemies of bats are probably the predatory hawks and owls; the day and nighttime "police forces" of birddom. Screech owls, among the smaller of American owls, are known to prey on bats; undoubtedly all owls do. It is unlikely that much predation is done by aerial chase; however agile the owl or hawk, the bat is master at abrupt turns and dodging. Any owl which might enter a cave, of course, would have a field day, but most bats probably are taken in hollow trees, the communal home of both pursuer and pursued. Some kinds of hawks, if flying early or very late (not a common occurrence with most varieties) are capable of

Macroglossus,
a Nectar-eating bat

taking bats in the air, particularly the slow-flying
species. And as is seen in so many cases, there is
a particular species—in this case a falcon—which
adapts itself to the point of having fairly exclusive
rights. The "bat falcon" *Machaerhamphus*, an
Old World tropical-forest species, has developed
quite large eyes through its habit of hunting not
only at dusk but even in the darkness of night. It
is known to outfly certain species of bats—even
the relatively swift-flying, narrow-winged *Mops*—
snatching them out of the air in its short-beaked,
very wide mouth. The victimized bats are swallowed whole while the bird is in the air. Other
falcons, kites, and hawks have been known to attack bats, particularly the cave species which
emerge in great, tightly packed numbers. These
birds of prey will swoop into such a bat cloud
and lash out in any direction, hardly capable of
missing. Unlike such kindergarten tactics are those
of the bat falcon, who deftly singles out individuals and outflies them. *Machaerhamphus*, however, though widely dispersed both in Africa and
throughout the tropical East, is rather uncommon
and hardly a threat to bats in any number.

Snakes are a hitherto unsuspected hazard, recent findings have borne out. Snakes of any
species are well-adapted to seek out and feed on
bats; possibly they are a more destructive enemy
of migrating bats than we even now are inclined
to believe. Certainly they prey upon bird nestlings
to a sobering degree. The tropical boas and
pythons are often specially adapted as bat-catchers
because of their climbing agility. A friend tells of
an exciting capture in Queensland, Australia.

He had been shooting at a rare variety of the
small, nectar-feeding bats (*Macroglossus*) which

were elusively darting round a flowering tree. He had failed, in the fast-fading light, to secure any specimens, but would have sworn, he said, that he had killed a bat with his last shot just as darkness fell. So certain was he that he looked for many minutes longer than he ordinarily would to find that "certain" bat. No bat came to light—but, while vainly looking, he came upon a carpet python and—being a scientist on an expedition—captured it and brought it into camp to the herpetologist. The snake was duly labeled, measured, sexed, and scale-counted—all common functions in snake study —and was then injected and placed in a formalin solution, i.e., "pickled," as the term goes. Many months later, back in America, the same snake was being studied and, upon dissection, was found to have a small bat in its stomach, also preserved, along with the snake. This bat, as a sort of bonus, was borne upstairs in the great museum to the desk of the man who had originally collected the snake. He found it to be of the same rare species at which he had shot that night and missed. Nor had he collected it subsequently on that expedition. Here was a splendid find! Everyone was delighted, and it made a good story. "But," he mused, "was this the bat he 'knew' he had shot, or another?" There were no marks or evident shot-holes in the bat, but he pursued it nontheless. This particular type was too rare a bat to go poking about in unless it was being seriously studied—a most time-consuming project—so instead he took it to a friend, a medical doctor, who X-rayed the tiny animal. Sure enough: a single lead pellet had reached the brain, probably through the roof of the mouth.

I have no such splendid tale to relate, but also in Queensland, on a later expedition, I found in the hot interior of a cave (a phenomenon in itself: caves are usually cool), on the rough stone ceiling, an Australian Brown Tree snake, *Boiga fusca,* dining most nobly on a small species of *Rhinolophus.* He had the further effrontery to have a bat in his mouth. Later, at camp in Einasleigh, the snake was found to have two more bats in his stomach.

The story of bats' enemies goes on. Merriam reported having seen large trout catch bats as they swept low over the water surface to drink. Certainly other such fish, particularly those in the pickerel or bass families, must take a certain toll. Allen mentions that possibly very large spiders may feed on the smaller bats . . . and, indeed, I have verified this by having seen a small bat (*Pipistrellus*) enmeshed in the web of the large New Guinea bird spider.

Still, with it all, bats—migratory or otherwise —have no enemy of an outstanding nature, other than man, the only apparent species whose mind is troubled by visions both real and unreal. Other mammal species, excepting man, though they have no lack of talents, have neither man's inventiveness, nor—it is perhaps fortunate—his unique forms of imagination.

15

Deep
Freeze

Migration and hibernation, though they rhyme, and are often lumped together for that reason, are at opposite poles. One might even construe them to be among the basic forces which prompted Isaac Walton's,

And for that I shall tell you, that in ancient times a debate hath risen . . . whether the happiness of man in this world doth consist more in Contemplation or Action.

Not that bats do much contemplating, but they do sense cold, and cold is the very essence of hibernation—from *hibernus*, "winter." We do know that bats hibernate and we must have known it from man's first housing quest having led him into a cave to find no one else at home. The principal force which led both species to seek such protection was cold. There is one major factor which separates bat from man in this problem of communal living: the bat undergoes a lowering of body temperature and slowing of functions—

190

somewhat of a death within life—which man has not been able to duplicate. Other mammals, too, possess this protective device; ground squirrels, the woodchuck, and various mice. It is cause for thought, since bats are, generally, a tropical type of mammal, that any of them should have survived the coming of cold (as it is believed to have come) which seems so neatly to have disposed of such apparent stalwarts as the dinosaurs. And why did not other kinds of bats seek the same solution? More than one researcher has come forward with the suggestion that bats may well have crossed into the New World via a warm belt and so never have had to flee the cold. But then, in such a case, why did certain species penetrate into the colder areas?

There has been a good deal of earnest research done on the faculty of suspension employed by bats. It is indicated now, in all species, that such states of being are brought about by the regulation of metabolic balance. There are those animal species which have a virtually constant metabolism; others, outwardly similar, are metabolically constructed to take on the temperature of their surroundings. This division is not always clearly defined; there are elaborate degrees of compromise. At one end there are the lizards, and at the other, man; the bats and other hibernating species seem to lie, metabolically, somewhere in between. As Griffin points out, even the species of most constant temperature yet retain a link with our reputed progenitors, as man, for instance, is subject to cold hands and feet. These extremities fall to much lower temperatures, yet survive. In hibernating species, the entire body falls in temperature. Metabolism, in itself, is the ratio of building to the destruction of protoplasmic cells, or, the ratio of heat energy taken in as oxygen and food to that expended. Increased activity burns more energy as an accelerated engine burns more fuel. In lizards, temperatures are equated as quickly as a chameleon changes color. In non-hibernating animals, metabolic reflexes control a heating and cooling mechanism less instantaneous in its effect. With bats, a system of more gradual reflexes is evident in any awakened bat, even in summer. But once awake he is very much awake.

In actual hibernation it is a more gradual process, beginning with the cooling of the air in autumn. The caves or places chosen for hibernation—and here "choose" is directly applied to the psychical discrimination of the bat—are, curiously, always at a constant temperature, which seldom falls below 42 degrees F. The bats, whose inner urge of instinctive reason led them to prepare by means of a deepening quiescence, are themselves cooled from a 104 degree peak, at height of action, to the low temperature whose general minimum is 42 degrees when they are in the depths of their long sleep.

Barbastella,
a bat of Great Britain
and Europe

Not all bats which hibernate remain in so deathlike a slumber. The "deep sleepers" are mostly of the *Vespertilionidae,* belonging to those genera which penetrate into the north temperate zones: *Myotis, Pipistrellus, Eptesicus,* and *Plecotus* in the New World, and *Myotis, Pipistrellus, Barbastella, Plecotus,* and *Miniopterus* in the Old. No reliable information is available for the south Temperate Zone. The "light sleepers" are some species of the Old World *Rhinolophidae* and the world-wide *Molossidae.* These latter are bats which hibernate in the comparatively more mild limits of 50 to 52 degrees F.

The deep sleepers are so profoundly unconscious that their respiration is hardly perceptible. Several minutes may pass, upon having been removed from their perches and warmed, before they exhibit any sign of life. Moisture often condenses on their fur in hoary beads and they hang suspended like so many soaked lumps of wool. The duration of this sleep is often regulated by the length of the winter, that is to say, the prolonged measure of temperatures at reasonably constant degrees of cold. Since the temperature of the cave is so uniformly constant and slow to show change, it is curious how bats awaken to an early spring, but they do. The fluctuations of spring activity vary, but little information has been compiled concerning how the bats perceive any change, temperatures, as I say, remaining constant.

What would happen if the temperature dropped below 42 degrees? Of course experiments have been tried. Below their normal minimum temperature bats were found to survive if slowly lowered to around 30 degrees. But "survival" in this case, being of course at a temperature below freezing, is simply a matter of prolonging the time when, as the metabolism and the combined forces of life-flow (many of them liquid) accelerate to keep up with the formation of ice crystals, they must gradually lose ground and decelerate to a point of clogging, so causing the animal to die. The ability to raise the level of heat production to offset any emergency has but a narrow margin, thus it is quite possible for hibernating bats sometimes to freeze to death. Degree points between 32 and 41 degrees F. are simply demarcations at which life is prolonged to a greater length, depending upon the stamina of the bat; 42 degrees is not an absolute minimum but that which is most conducive to survival over a long period. If much lower temperatures are to be endured apparently it will be only by another period of acclimatization. If the hibernating bat is exposed to drastic changes of temperature it is as prone to pneumonia and allied congestive ailments as any bat at normal temperatures. Where many bats congregate a higher body temperature is maintained for longer periods than in individuals, but this temperature lowers in relative proportion to the numbers involved, finally reaching the temperature of the cave.

Besides temperature reduction, the mucous lining of the larynx and windpipe increases in the deep-sleeping bats to the degree of restricting air passage, thus reducing oxygen intake, and breathing is reduced from a rate of around 200 intakes and expulsions per minute, to a low of 23 per minute, with periodic cycles of extremely low counts of one breath in only every three to eight minutes! (Swanson and Evans). But the principal point of importance is that the bat enters the cave with a great proportion of fat, and this cushion of "food" or heat energy is expended at low volume as the winter wanes, and the animal emerges with virtually no fat at all, losing over one third in total weight. The light sleepers have no such drastic reactions, but, although in the sound sleep of actual hibernation, are easily awakened and quickly restored to all of their natural functions. Neither group takes food during its long period of inactivity, and the bowels appear to cease entirely in their functions.

The period of awakening is relative to the two groups mentioned and to their comparative lengths of hibernation. During an exceptionally mild winter there is a degree of unrest and semi-awakening in many individuals long before there is a general awakening. When it does come, there appear to be four discernible stages: (1) a deep sleep, with almost no response to handling, (2) slight, and very slow, extensions of the hind limbs (the so-called "hanging reflex," which will take place even after the forepart of the brain is removed), (3) more pedal and manual movement begins, also there is a beginning of vocal sounds, and, (4) full comprehension and reflexes (Merzbacher). None of these stages is distinctly noticeable but they merge one into the other, as one feeds the other on a slightly higher temperature, until full activity restores normality in temperature and action. The conclusion that the poor beast must be devilishly hungry is theoretically applicable, but there does not appear to be any rush for the outside world. Even when fully alert, upon being awakened, the bats seem to spend a certain amount of time on trial flights within the cave, in quarreling, and in reshuffling their groups. I have seen, besides, more than one enormous, healthy yawn!

The winters in the middle-eastern United States are long and often cold. The snow, if not at all times deep, is quite deep enough, and unlike the true northeast of New England, has a tendency often to be neither snow nor ice but a viscous, icy porridge. Even with bare patches of earth showing, one steps in and out of this chilling mire with unavoidable constancy. The wind is not severe but it blows from every direction with all the comfort of a cold wet towel. It was in this less-than-Paradise that my own interest in bats was initiated.

My first bat quest was deep inside, not a cave, but an abandoned iron mine. I had heard romantic tales of this mine; it had been one of the sources of cannon balls during the Revolutionary War and, it was related, was hardly changed since that era. Bats were said to hang in thousands from the tunnel ceiling. This was all too much to bear, so the very next Saturday found two hot-eyed youths pedaling furiously on bicycles the long eighteen miles to the mine. It was, I remember, the most lowering of February days, penetratingly cold and damp. We straggled home at nine o'clock at night, half-frozen and exhausted, and arrived to be read a parental riot act of no inconsiderable dimension. But it was a glorious experience; and though I have since been to some wild places I cannot think that the thrill of exploration has ever been more vividly electrifying than on that first day. We returned with a half dozen bats, studied their every part, and gloried in them. Still schoolboys, however, we could not resist a bit of fun. Entirely too full of ourselves, we took the bats to the Claridge Theater in Montclair and set them loose (they having been most unceremoniously jarred from their deep sleep). As poor Mr. Karloff (or someone very like him) was struggling through all the usual stiff-jointed, stake-through-the-neck routine, our bats, circling high under the vault of the theater, reached the beam of light issuing from the projection booth, and suddenly flashed their shadows twenty feet wide on the screen, causing pandemonium! I remember the teams of prim ushers rushing up and down the aisles, their lights flashing on and off, trying to calm the audience. How we hooted! But an elderly white-haired lady who sat in front of me became terribly upset and had to leave. That took all the wind out of my sails, and I felt shabby and mean. Later, confronting my mother, I was not only read a lesson in manners but re-

DEEP
FREEZE
197

it seem
were d
lars of
few hu
deathles
entranc
mens o
Often f
more of
The m
the Litt
seeming
they hu
gray sto
entrance
ward for
their nu
Myotis l
very sim
Eastern
must be
parison;
(but not
appears
infreque
Myotis s
first two,
black ma
with his
found, in
specimen
Northeas
than Myo
a variega
dition, its
or pinkis
Our sm

minded that my beloved bats would now not only certainly die, but that in so using them I had robbed them of their dignity. "Dignity," at that age, was but a vaguely defined concept most poorly formulated. I puzzled over it and emerged with a freshened understanding which I have had little cause to alter. I ended up apologizing to the manager, and to this day have never forgotten the profound lesson in compassion which was revealed to me. Some considerable number of Saturdays later (for more was applied than parental reproof) two chastened, but still earnest, boys were back at the same mine to begin that which evolved into serious study. I banded my first bats there and for some years returned each winter as faithfully as the bats.

Just last January, some twenty-five years later, I again returned to that old mine. This time instead of arriving half-frozen on a rime-coated bicycle, I emerged from a warm car in company with a contingent of scientists down from Harvard, carrying such an assortment of electronic devices, flash cameras, special cages, and general paraphernalia as to intimidate the most nonchalant lay observer. I was amazed to find that not one thing had changed, not only within the mine, but in the strong, oak-bristled landscape, the rocky escarpments, and even in the old general store with its glassed-in penny candy; everything remained the same. Only our new model cars clashed with the solemn winter tranquility and quiet aura of the past.

Nor had the bats changed. Still were they there in thousands—twenty thousand, we judged, by careful estimate. Upon entering the mine we found it warm compared with the frigid outside world, but though 42 degrees is warmer than 20

it seemed chill enough and damp, and the bats
were deep in slumber. Great stalactites and pillars of ice had formed near the entrance, but a
few hundred feet inside the mine there was the
deathless perpetuity of the catacombs. Near the
entrance we found, as always, individual specimens of *Eptesicus fuscus*, the Big Brown bat.
Often found in numbers in houses, *Eptesicus* is
more often a solitary inhabitant in eastern caves.
The most common species is *Myotis lucifugus*,
the Little Brown bat. In phalanx after phalanx,
seeming like withered, closely packed brown leaves,
they hung in festoons from the cold crevices of
gray stone. They are not with *Eptesicus* at the
entrance, but are seen only as one proceeds inward for at least two or three hundred feet. Then,
their numbers are staggering. Beside the common
Myotis lucifugus lucifugus, there is often another
very similar, *Myotis keenii septentrionalis*, the
Eastern Long-eared Brown bat. The two species
must be laid side by side for an adequate comparison; in *keenii* the ears are perceptibly longer
(but not to any startling degree) and the color
appears just slightly brighter. Also, there is not
infrequently to be found the Least Brown bat,
Myotis subulatus leibii; much smaller than the
first two, and with not only a rather raccoonlike
black mask but also a peculiar way of hanging
with his wings slightly akimbo. Besides these, we
found, in vaulted chambers off the main tunnel,
specimens of *Pipistrellus subflavus obscurus*, the
Northeastern Pipistrelle bat. This slightly less
than *Myotis*-sized bat is rather prettily coated in
a variegated tricolor yellowish-brown fur. In addition, its forearms are nearly always of a reddish
or pinkish hue in contrast with *Myotis'* black.

Our small, short-lived, but still valid "expedition" proceeded to count, photograph, make electronic experiments, take temperatures, specimens, and records of every species in the mine. Many banded bats were noted and recorded. The species I have described from this single mine, with the inclusion of the three migratory species of which we have spoken, are virtually all of the bats found in the northeastern United States. Upon rare occasions a more southerly species or subspecies of *Myotis* will be found, but none other than these mentioned seem about to adapt themselves for survival in so cold a climate.

As our party concluded its work and again wriggled out into the open air, we found that the temperature had sharply decreased as night had fallen. The patches of mud through which we had walked in coming had turned iron-hard and rang now with our footsteps. The moon was bright as midday but appeared as comfortless as a glowing ice sphere in an ice-encrusted world. We remarked that, however chilled and damp the mine, the bats seemed, by comparison, to have a haven both snug and protected.

Banding of cave bats, begun only a few years before I first "discovered" my mine, gained in impetus and direction with the years. Caves and mines and fissures throughout the northeast were carefully searched out by mammalogists and speleologists through such sources as old Revolutionary maps and reports of geological surveys. Soon banding began to reveal information hitherto unimagined. Local migrations of whole bat populations were traced from winter hibernation caves to summer quarters in other caves or barns or church belfries many miles away. Also homing studies brought interesting results. It was found that bats were able to find their way home after having been taken as far away as 180 miles. And even when taken 25 miles out to sea aboard a ship, the bats could still unerringly fly back to the home roost. Certainly this instinct, found in many animal species, seems not in any way connected with audio-perception. It seems, rather, to be somehow linked to the same equations which coordinate gravitational and celestial movements. All within that tiny box of a brain! Further, ages in certain of these species, notably *Myotis*, have been verified by banding to reach a known extreme of over twenty years. Even an average span must be at least twelve or fifteen years, for bats banded over twelve years before have been found pregnant or with nursing young.

We have gone on at some length about hibernation and its general application to bats in one of the more frigid parts of the north Temperate Zone. But Kentucky, for instance, is far less hibernian than Maine, and Georgia, even in the mountains, is even less so. What of hibernating bats in these areas? It goes back entirely to the root of the word: if there is enough "winter" or cold, bats metabolically prepared to hibernate will do so. Very often they sleep, but not as deeply. In the warmer parts of their ranges they do not hibernate at all.

What, however, of those bats found in tropical caves which are often found to be, if not hibernating, at least excessively quiescent? I think that, beyond much doubt, these bats are possibly possessed of such a metabolic structure as to be able to "fast," or at least to rest, for long periods, occasioned by adverse weather, as in monsoon seasons, or periodic fluctuations in a staple food supply. There is another term occasionally used— as I believe I mentioned in discussing migration is a general awakening. When it does come, there appear to be four discernible stages: (1) a deep sleep, with almost no response to handling, (2) slight, and very slow, extensions of the hind limbs (the so-called "hanging reflex," which will take place even after the forepart of the brain is removed), (3) more pedal and manual movement begins, also there is a beginning of vocal sounds, and, (4) full comprehension and reflexes (Merzbacher). None of these stages is distinctly noticeable but they merge one into the other, as one feeds the other on a slightly higher temperature, until full activity restores normality in temperature and action. The conclusion that the poor beast must be devilishly hungry is theoretically applicable, but there does not appear to be any rush for the outside world. Even when fully alert, upon being awakened, the bats seem to spend a certain amount of time on trial flights within the cave, in quarreling, and in reshuffling their groups. I have seen, besides, more than one enormous, healthy yawn!

The winters in the middle-eastern United States are long and often cold. The snow, if not at all times deep, is quite deep enough, and unlike the true northeast of New England, has a tendency often to be neither snow nor ice but a viscous, icy porridge. Even with bare patches of earth showing, one steps in and out of this chilling mire with unavoidable constancy. The wind is not severe but it blows from every direction with all the comfort of a cold wet towel. It was in this less-than-Paradise that my own interest in bats was initiated.

My first bat quest was deep inside, not a cave, but an abandoned iron mine. I had heard romantic tales of this mine; it had been one of the

sources of cannon balls during the Revolutionary
War and, it was related, was hardly changed since
that era. Bats were said to hang in thousands from
the tunnel ceiling. This was all too much to bear,
so the very next Saturday found two hot-eyed
youths pedaling furiously on bicycles the long
eighteen miles to the mine. It was, I remember,
the most lowering of February days, penetratingly
cold and damp. We straggled home at nine
o'clock at night, half-frozen and exhausted, and
arrived to be read a parental riot act of no inconsiderable dimension. But it was a glorious experience; and though I have since been to some
wild places I cannot think that the thrill of exploration has ever been more vividly electrifying
than on that first day. We returned with a half
dozen bats, studied their every part, and gloried
in them. Still schoolboys, however, we could not
resist a bit of fun. Entirely too full of ourselves,
we took the bats to the Claridge Theater in Montclair and set them loose (they having been most
unceremoniously jarred from their deep sleep).
As poor Mr. Karloff (or someone very like him)
was struggling through all the usual stiff-jointed,
stake-through-the-neck routine, our bats, circling
high under the vault of the theater, reached the
beam of light issuing from the projection booth,
and suddenly flashed their shadows twenty feet
wide on the screen, causing pandemonium! I remember the teams of prim ushers rushing up
and down the aisles, their lights flashing on and
off, trying to calm the audience. How we hooted!
But an elderly white-haired lady who sat in front
of me became terribly upset and had to leave.
That took all the wind out of my sails, and I felt
shabby and mean. Later, confronting my mother,
I was not only read a lesson in manners but re-

—that is, "over-winter," which might be applied to a migratory bat such as the Silver-haired, individuals of which are known not to migrate and still survive. In such cases, I will venture a guess —for it is no more—that the Silver-haired bat *does* go into partial hibernation, at least; in much the same way my tame tropical cockatoo, if gradually permitted to do so, will become able to withstand subfreezing temperatures. I was amazed, only last winter, to visit a friend who had an unheated outdoor aviary simply alive with singing canaries at a temperature of 20 degrees F. Again, during the winter just past, I was called to the telephone in January to "please help with a bat which is flying round the kitchen." I arrived to find a plump and saucy Silver-hair, most thoroughly waked up and active. It was related that the bat had been "living on spiders" in the basement. I doubt that—but what, exactly, it did do, I do not know. Most probably, having settled down in a cool corner to pass the winter, it may have been warmed by some air draft from the heating system, and, thus having been awakened, began to fly about.

Unlike the hyperborean lemmings and certain hibernating bats, I am a "warmth lover." I prefer the long, scented, tropical nights and the warm seas glowing with phosphorescence and starlight. But I have known times when the winter moon was bright and the snow "sang" underfoot in the dry cold of a deep January night; when the spruces and balsams echoed to a lynx cry and . . . as Robert Frost so softly sang it:

. . . When there was no more lantern in the kitchen,
The fire got out through crannies in the stove
And danced in yellow wrigglers on the ceiling,
As much at home as if they'd always danced there.

Soon there will be another massing of bats at that mine about which I spoke. There will be another great falling of leaves; sumac and swamp maples and blueberries first, as they always go. The wind will begin to bite and the mud ruts will freeze and be, as John Buchan has had it, "lemon-colored in the sunset . . . when the noble bones of the land are bare and you get the essential savor of earth and wood and water." It seems only fitting that this place be called Hibernia. And it is.

16

Noctes
Ambrosianae

Having just released you from the dark under-world of a cave—and a frigid one at that —I am about to plunge you into yet others. It is just so in exploring caves: one often comes up into the warm sunshine swearing an end to it, and an hour later is down inside another. The fascination which caves hold for the casual amateur sometimes verges on the morbid, a taste, as it were, of the sepulcher; a sort of "House of Horror" in which to have a mild dalliance with the macabre. But serious speleologists are a healthy and vigorous breed; they more often than not have earnest business in which the thrill of exploration is far outweighed by more pressing matters. Geologists, ichthyologists, entomologists, virologists, botanists, mammalogists—even skin divers—all of these are bound to haunt caves from time to time. In point of fact, caves are no more than holes in the ground. Any benefit derived from them or their contents must come from within ourselves.

Caves are not always cold, as were those from which we have just come. Many are warm, even hot. Some are well-ventilated and refreshing, while others are stifling. Some caves are so deep and so large as to defy description, while others are simply fissures or clefts. In America, the Carlsbad Caverns in New Mexico and Mammoth Cave, Wyandotte, and Luray Caverns in the east, are examples of the larger and more well-known caves. In South America, Humboldt's "Cavern of the Guacharos" is a noted cave, and in Europe Gauffre Berger, the Lascaux, Eisreisenwelt, and Capri's famed Blue Grotto are all a happy playground for speleologists. In 1954 a party of cave explorers descended to a record depth of 3,000 feet near Grenoble, France, and only recently that depth has been exceeded. Asia and Australia have their caves, and New Zealand's Waitomo Cave is lighted by the phosphoresence of a million glow-worms. There are limestone, granite, basalt, and gypsum caves, lava caves, ice caves, and sea caves. And bats inhabit them all.

Bats use caves for hibernation only where hibernation is necessary. Otherwise caves are used simply as "houses." In some caves, such as our own Carlsbad Caverns, literally millions of bats congregate, the greater number in this case being *Tadarida mexicana*, the Mexican Free-tailed bat. Also found in great numbers in caves are the *Miniopterinae, Hipposideridae, Rhinolophidae,* and some of the *Pteropodidae* in southeastern Asia and Australasia.

My own experiences have led me into some weird situations. I have been wedged into nearly inextricable positions in rock chimneys, bruised and scraped and lacerated in clinging to cavernous heights, and nearly suffocated in long, foot-high tunnels, as my body blocked air passage and I lay exhausted from continued efforts. I remember the great, vaulted ceiling of a cave which was situated on an isolated island in the Solomon Sea. There appeared to be ten thousand burning coals looking back at me as I cast my torch on the great masses of bats high over my head. The eyes reflected my light in shimmering waves as the bats blinked or turned away, and I remember the odd sensation I felt as I recalled that I was quite alone not only under tons of stone but surrounded by thousands of square miles of alien water. And in another cave—a limestone cave on Sudest Island off the coast of New Guinea —we found so many bats (*Miniopterus*) that the wind blast and thunder of their emergence was like standing near the back flow of a jet engine. Yet another New Guinea cave, at Ehaus on Misima Island, was more fabulously beautiful than any I ever before had seen: there were great domes, apses, arches, and vaulted ceilings colored in pastel shades of pink, rose, and white, and there were deep, limpid pools of water which varied from tender greens to the majestic velvet blue-green of a tropic midnight. I so vividly remember the entrance to that cave: it was "puri-puri," or black magic, to the natives, and they would not approach it; we had to lie on our backs in a three-inch stream of water and lower ourselves into the darkness upside down as it were, and backward as well, through a foot-high aperture which for all the world looked like a whale's mouth! Neither shall I forget the return: from the cool, antiseptic, refrigeratorlike depths, we emerged into the warm, sun-drenched, humid, aromatic grandeur of what was literally a forest of orchids! But wherever they are located and whatever kinds of bats inhabit

Aselliscus,
a rare Horseshoe bat

them, caves have one thing in common: they are an alien world from which, however earnest our pursuits, we are always glad to return.

With all the spiraling grandeur of form and color so often found in bat caves, there is quite often another commodity, far more "earthy" in nature. We have all heard of it: "guano" is the term most often applied, at least in reference to the substance as a product of commercial value. This natural product, from many sources, is salable to a world-wide market still, although chemical fertilizers are beginning to make inroads. The early Peruvians seem to have known about it for centuries, but it was not until 1804, when Alexander von Humboldt returned with samples from his South American travels, that Europeans (again, meaning ourselves) first discovered its immense value to agriculture.

Most natural guano used commercially comes from the great bird islands off the coast of Peru, where millions of sea birds roost and perpetually renew the supply. There are literally mountains of it, and guano is one of the major bulwarks to Peruvian prosperity. The essence of value in guano is its high content of nitrogen and phosphates, invaluable agents in soil renewal. Generally, its form in a natural state is a brownish powder, very much caked or compressed, and with a smell more musty, "acid," than anything more profound. In many bat caves I have sunk to my knees in this brown powder, which, although essentially inoffensive, is often poor footing, as in clambering over piled bales of peat moss.

Bat guano is an equally marketable—often highly profitable—commercial product. A spectacular demonstration of its value was the commencement of operations in 1957 on a guano dis-

Facing page:
Snap-shooting
tropical bats

covery in a cave deep at Granite Gorge in the Grand Canyon. The original estimate was in the vicinity of 100,000 tons at a total worth of fifteen million dollars! The guano was sucked into great buckets, each with a capacity of 3,500 pounds, by an enormous vacuum pump, and was removed by aerial tramway. The retail price was $1.10 for five pounds, put up in neat packages like so much flour. The difficulty of access encountered at Granite Gorge is typical of the problems that the removal of bat guano entails. Seldom is it in an accessible spot for commercial advantage. I have seen thousands of tons which may never be used.

But why, on such a chapter, do I tack so seemingly irrelevant a title as "Ambrosial Nights"? I will tell you. It is because in working with bats one has cause to remember, not the dank, musk-permeated, fear-crowded pit of Stygian darkness that is a cave, nor the occasional horrors of pestilence in the humid tropics where bats abound; rather one's lasting impression is of wonder and awe at the magnitude and grandeur of the forces which so combine, multiply, disintegrate, dissolve, unite, and procreate to ends which lie beyond one's comprehension. Bats, like anything else, are only measurable in relation to one's knowledge of them. I do not mean knowledge learned from books whose aim is to sublimate your thinking, but actual knowledge applicable only through the senses. Certainly neither sublimation nor even persuasion is within the bounds of this endeavor. I can only tell you about that which has been my experience. And my own experience with bats has brought me both pleasure and pain. There are few tales of adventure or derring-do; rather, it has been a quiet kind of quest. I suppose that if one is bound up with machinery there is an underlying "thumpa-ta, thumpa-ta" with which one must keep in rhythm or fall behind. Bats demand no such keeping-in-step. My recollections are of calm, windless evenings in which one watches the stars "turn on" as if by mercury switches and the fading cloud tints seem to race for the horizon as a mouse streaks for its hole. Duck hunters and other sportsmen—yachtsmen, too—will know my feelings in this. So, perhaps, will you.

There is sport from time to time. Bats are not easy to knock out of the sky. C. Hart Merriam has stated that, "though I have been fortunate enough to shoot fourteen Hoary bats, I would rather kill another than slay a dozen deer." So would I; more so, in that I have never shot a Hoary bat. Hoary bats are fast, agile, and usually fly only in the gloom of night. I have tried, by starlight, and missed. I shall try again.

But it is not the sport of bats which holds my interest, but the animals themselves. I repeat, a bat has but to be a bat. There is a whole procession of lizards, tigers, pangolins, aardvarks, monkeys, tropical fish, wines, heiroglyphics, paintings, foods, beautiful women, rockets, Grecian ruins, and what-not-a-jumble of interesting things, all pounding through the world at the same time. How does one choose? One doesn't. There is not time, by half. One just muddles through, I think, picking a little here, gleaning a little there. Bats, too, are part of it all.

17

My Friend Freddie Craig

There is a trading center on the southeastern tip of New Guinea, called Samarai. Among its leading citizens is a most enterprising, sound, and virile gentleman, whose name is Freddie Craig. To his intimates, however, or occasionally heard shouted above the lusty Australian voices at the cricket field, there is another name by which he is known: "Flying Fox." Now this is an odd name, at least so used, and it is often wondered how it was acquired. The answer is amusing but simple.

Freddie, as a younger man, had often to travel by sea, frequently on copra schooners, which both reek and roll with little thought to queasy stomachs. Freddie's solution, to his stomach's ease, was to eat nothing while at sea but tinned fruit; it grew dull, but the sea lost its misery for him. Now of course, in any port, there are always those with cast-iron stomachs who hoot aloud at the faintest tinge of green in anyone. In this case they were no doubt chagrined about Freddie's cure, so they began immediately to rag him about something else. Tinned fruit? Who eats fruit? Flying Foxes. And so "Flying Fox" Craig it became and so it remains.

Having known Freddie Craig and liked him enormously, and having been filled with at least a dozen beer-glossed accounts of his acquired nickname, when a few years later I came upon a young flying fox and kept it as a pet, by a sort of poetic justice there was no hesitation whatever about calling it "Freddie Craig."

I first saw Freddie—the fruit bat—hanging on a telephone wire under a blazing sun, at Karumba, a settlement on the shores of the Gulf of Carpentaria. Politically, Karumba is in northern Queensland, Australia, but few Australians have ever seen it, for it is about as isolated as a place can be and still cling to this earth. We had been "bush" at this time for some three months and, since it was our business to do so, had seen just about every living thing in that part of the world. We had had more than a bit of hard luck with numbers of animals, for it was in the "dry" and the land was as parched as our throats. We had water bags tied on the hood of our incredibly dirt-caked Land Rover—ostensibly to cool by evaporation, but they, too, were so thickly caked that they had the look of sun-glazed pottery. We had ground to a dust-choked stop in order to kick the bags free, when we met Freddie.

Since I was particularly interested in bats, I must say in truth, we had not let much in the bat line slip by. We had captured the Horseshoe bat, Spear-nosed bats, Long-eared bats, Wattled bats, Broad-nosed bats, Bent-winged bats, Free-tailed bats, and, as I have already related, even *Macroderma*, the "Ghost" bat. But in that arid country

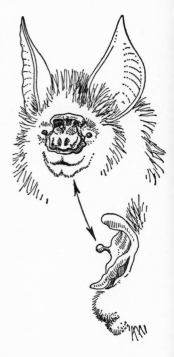

Hipposideros stenotis, an Australian Horseshoe bat

of "black soil" plains, in which the only relief from the hot gravel and talcum-powder-like sand, the gray-green mulga, and the saltbush and spinifex, was the occasional river bottom oasis, fruit bats were a rarity. Far from the southern orchards and the eastern rain forests, the *Pteropodidae*, though never common, were to be found in any numbers only during the "wet" when the desert sprang to life. During the rest of the year they were only occasional rovers among the tea trees and gums or the crocodile-infested river bottoms, or skulkers amid the mangroves on the Gulf. We had tried at rare intervals to collect an odd specimen or two which we happened on by accident. In all cases luck had been against us. Our bat "record" was enviable, but there was an irritating gap—and that was *Pteropus gouldii*. Since the region had been so little explored zoologically, we particularly wanted a specimen to see if there might not be a possible subspecies of the eastern form. We thirsted to bridge that infuriating gap.

And there, hanging on a telephone wire, was our bat. We had stopped on that incendiary bit of road, as I have said, to free our water bags. Lionel hissed, "There he sits, mate," and reached for his gun as I reached for mine. Bill, eager to be in on it all, breathlessly dove for his camera. All of this, mind you, for a bat which ordinarily is by no means uncommon. Poor fellow, he just happened to be in demand and we'd had a full six hours of tooth-jarring jounces and were in need of exercise. Eager as dingoes scenting a carcass, we crept ever closer in the fashion of moviedom's villains attacking a stagecoach, with grave admonitions to "go easy," and (from me) "Don't shoot till you see the whites of his eyes," which made no more sense to my Australian friends than Mat-

thew Flinders does to you. Grown-ups playing the
fool: generally a costly venture. I was closer; I
drew a careful aim and mentally covered every
air route—was just about to shout out (having a
psychic dislike for "sitting ducks")—when the bat
winked at me! I saw he was a baby and shouted to
the others to hold off. We walked up under him
and there he hung, just as his mother had left
him. He swung first on one foot then on the
other, in idle convolutions, fanning himself with
a lackadaisical wing. His bright eyes sparkled and
blinked. Lionel took aim with a stick and, after
three misses and considerable picturesque comment, knocked Freddie galley-west, spinning him
down like a parachute.

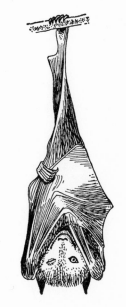

Freddie landed in a bush, and we closed in,
all loudly shouting advice about the length,
breadth, and probable sharpness of his teeth.
Reaching the bush we reacted to Freddie as we
might have to a tiger snake, gingerly cautious at
very least. But Freddie gave us a good-natured
squeak and solved the problem by playfully crawl-
ing up my shirt front and tucking his head under
my arm. This elicited a tremendous howl from
Lionel, who laughed himself to tears, saying,
"Oh, but my bloody oath, mate, you do make a
rollickin' good mother!" Bill lay on the ground
convulsed and there I was, mother to it.

Anxious to be out of the heat and into the
Normanton pub at sundown, we popped Freddie
into a small cage and there he hung, swaying like

a pendulum and absorbing every giant jounce of the truck far better than we. Halfway back we stopped to capture a monitor lizard for Bill (who was our herpetologist), and while resting after the fruitful but exhausting chase, Lionel tried out Freddie on some tinned fruit cocktail ("being a flaming fruit bat," said Lionel). Freddie ate it with relish, and we were off in another dust cloud with our adopted baby, whose little stomach was a virtual pot-belly of tinned fruit.

Freddie had joined us at a period of boredom and lackluster. Usually, with any such wild and reckless notion of the moment there is a considerable letdown the next morning; one often wishes that he'd let well enough alone and "had never seen the damned thing." But Freddie cast no pall; he remained healthy and hungry and as cheerful as a cricket. He simply "signed on" with the expedition and continued to bump and swing and chirrup and simply bubble over with good humor.

We had needs to discuss business, however. Here was the variety of *Pteropus* we had sought, only he was not a museum specimen. "What if he ran off," we thought. "Oh well, he'll probably die," I said, "they usually do." Then, all of us, looking back at that bouncing, ricocheting, pot-bellied bit of good will and sunshine, his eyes glistening as he "talked" to us, felt like murderers and drove on in silence. We were calloused enough, or had learned to be; killing animals was our business—and never mind the "good cause" behind it: killing is killing, no matter how it is painted. Fortunately, a day or so later, Lionel came in with a dead specimen and an enormous grin, saying, "Well, Freddie's off the hook!" Poor Freddie—not having been able to read our

Facing page:
Pteropus gouldii,
"Freddie Craig"

thoughts, he went on loving us all, especially his "mother."

At our various camps, as we stopped traveling and scientifically explored a given area, Freddie would make himself completely at home. He would hang near us on a bush, eat his fruit cocktail with us, and sleep contentedly on a roof support in the Land Rover. He had, like all of the *Pteropodidae*, a musky scent, but somehow he smelled not bad at all—"at least as good," said Lionel, "as we did." He would never "scurry" after the fashion of some bats, but would "walk." With a most deliberate and purposeful dignity, he would walk up and down and around you, would sit on your arm, look up into your eyes, and "talk.'" If you spoke in a monosyllable, Freddie would answer in a monosyllable. If you spoke a sentence, so would Freddie. And Freddie could "curse and swear" most admirably—which made him a "proper Aussie," Lionel said. I do not mean to anthropomorphize the poor devil. I do mean, however, to "canomorphize" if there is (which I doubt) any such word. This bat not only looked but behaved like a diminutive dog. Your dog does all of these things I mention, but a bat going through such homely, fireside routines, is amusing to a very great degree—even to Lionel, who was born among them and who, ordinarily, treats them with a disdain equivalent to the American farmer's contempt for a ground hog.

Freddie had the usual bat trait of perpetually cleaning himself. He would spend long periods licking his fur and kneading his rubbery membranes. He would stretch the wing membrane over his head, outlining his skull, as one might with a rubber sheet. Being a bat he would beat his wings furiously in imitation, as Lionel beat the brim of his felt hat to "sound like a flying fox." (Evidently he did.) Freddie seemed to be able to fly well enough, but seemed to prefer going nowhere. I shall never forget the time when, in stretching his wing over his head, he peeked out with one eye, hid back under, peeked yet again, then chittered at us! Of course, and I say this with all my belief, any such action is entirely accidental. I do not believe, indeed, I am certain, the bat has no cognizance of being amusing, as does a dog which perceives that a trick is entertaining and repeats it over and over for that reason. But it *appeared* that the bat thought it amusing, and we were compelled to laugh because it struck some sympathetic chord in us.

Freddie's painstaking toilet, his dining habits (in which he would deftly "lick his chops" and occasionally "slurp" his fruit juices), his irresistible expressions (from sleepy-eyed innocence to sparkle-eyed mischief), his "talking" and yawning—all were amusing to us. But his procedure in defecating was more hilarious than any other. He would change from his generically proper upside down position to hang by his thumbs. Having finished, he would simply turn round again. But to urinate, he would not only change round and hang by his thumbs (in which position, for some reason, he looked inordinately silly, anyway), but, having finished, he would shake his hips with some vigor as in a South American dance step, then resume his normal position with such a look of smugness and satisfaction as to convulse anyone who can remember training a two-year-old boy!

Freddie remained with us for nearly two months and grew to be a strapping youth. He never lost his pleasant disposition and became, if anything, more tame and companionable. But that phase of the expedition came abruptly to an end. We had to leave for New Guinea, and quarantine laws forbade Freddie's going along. Since my wife had flown up to Cairns for a short holiday before we were again to leave, she agreed, but with considerable reluctance—not knowing Freddie—to take him back home to Brisbane. Never have I seen so cautious and doubtful a meeting as that in which Barbara met Freddie. She approached him as though he were a hot coal. But Freddie's effervescent good humor promptly dispelled all fear. And when he licked her hand, she was captured. She flew off with Freddie on her lap, in a cage disguised with brown paper and topped with a spray of orchids, for the airline took a dim view of animals in the passenger compartment. Her description of the flight—told to me later—was that she had a seat next to a pleasant, but garrulous, elderly lady, who kept insisting she be shown the "bird"; she could not quite tell, she kept repeating, whether it was a canary or a parakeet. Freddie "sang" during the entire trip, and Barbara, who did not dare unveil him, fearing to cause someone heart failure if not pandemonium in the entire aircraft, had shamefacedly to endure the lady's injured feelings all the way home.

What of the Happy Ending? There is none. Freddie is dead, of course. Barbara kept him a full month, then, during a period of unseasonable cold weather he caught cold and she delivered him to an "expert" for proper care. With "proper" care he developed pneumonia and died.

There is no Moral to Freddie Craig. I was happy to have known him. You, too, will remember such "pets." They are never that, really, only captives.

Those which we think "amusing" are only natural actions seen through our eyes—eyes which see only that which we wish them to see. I carry a small medallion on which is engraved a simple statement by the noted explorer, the late Vilhjalmur Stefansson: ADVENTURES ARE A MARK OF INCOMPETENCE. Stefansson's meaning was not a scientist's lofty arrogance directed at you and me, we who might have romantic notions of exploring on our own. Rather, as he explained it, it was more a plea that we all exercise extreme care in preparation, to seek out knowledge and direction, before plunging headlong into the Unknown. Bats are to most people what the Arctic was, initially, to Stefansson: a Terra Incognita, beyond experience and beyond desire. Stefansson learned to know the Arctic and to love it, but although he lived there for long periods, he never chose to stay permanently. Why? Because the true Arctic is a realm beyond the normal sphere of man. So, also, are bats.

I can think of nothing to say by way of conclusion. Bats are bats; what we think of them has very little bearing on any of it. Perhaps we have come to know them somewhat better than we did before. There are scientists, as I have said, who are working in most earnest fashion to know more about bats. I am curious myself, and perhaps you will be. But scientists do indeed go to such a bother, do they not? One wonders whether, in the end, past generic taxonomy, metabolic vicissitudes, and genetic machinations, there may not be an answer even beyond their scope...

> Ah, said the little Leather-wingèd bat,
> I'll tell you the reason that,
> The reason that I fly in the night—
> Is because I lost my heart's delight.
> —AUTHOR UNKNOWN

Bibliography

Allen, Arthur A.: "Banding Bats," *Journ. Mammalogy*, 2, 1921.

Allen, G. M.: "Bats," Harvard University Press, Cambridge, Mass., 1939.

Allen, J. A., Herbert Lang, and James Chapin, "Congo Expedition, Collection of Bats," *Bull. Amer. Mus. Nat. Hist.*, New York, Vol. 37, Art. 18, 1917.

Anderson, Knud, "Catalogue of the Chiroptera in the Collection of the British Museum," Vol. 1, 1912.

Anthony, Harold E., "Field Book of North American Mammals," Putnam, New York, 1928.

———, "The Indigenous Land Mammals of Porto Rico, Living and Extinct," 2, New York, 1918.

Bailey, Vernon, "Animal Life of the Carlsbad Caverns," *Am. Soc. Mammal.*, No. 3, 1928.

Barrett, C. L., "An Australian Animal Book," Oxford Univ. Press, Oxford, 1947.

Benedict, J. E., "Notes on the Feeding Habits of *Noctilio*," *Journ. Mammalogy*, 7, 1926.

Bloedel, P., "Observations on the Life Histories of Panama Bats," *Journ. Mammalogy*, 36, 1955.

Cain, A. J., "Animal Species and Their Evolution," Hutchison, London, 1954.

Chapin, James P., "The Birds of the Belgian Congo," *Bull. Am. Mus. Nat. Hist.*, 65, 1932.

Chasen, F. N., "A Handlist to Malaysian Mammals," *Bull. Raffles Museum*, No. 15, Singapore, 1940.

Chubb, E. C., "The Mammals of Matabeleland," *Proc. Zool. Soc.*, London, 1909.

Cockrum, E. L., "Homing Movements and Longevity in Bats," *Journ. Mammalogy*, 37, 1956.

Dawson, W. R., "Bats as *Materia Medica*," *Ann. Mag. Nat. Hist.*, 16, 1925.

Derrennes, Charles, "The Life of the Bat," Butterworth, London, 1925.

Dobson, G.E., "Monograph of the Asiatic Chiroptera," Indian Museum, 1876.

Eisentraut, Martin, "Aus dem Leben der Fledermäuse und Flughunde," Verlag, Jena, 1957.

Ellerman, J. R. and T. C. S. Morrison-Scott, "Checklist of Paleoarctic and Indian Mammals," 1758–1951, British Museum (N.H.), London, 1951.

Ellerman, J. R. and T. C. S. Morrison-Scott and R. W. Hayman, "Southern African Mammals 1758 to 1951: A Reclassification," British Museum (N.H.), London, 1953.

Flower, W. H., "Osteology of the Mammalia," Macmillan, London, 1885.

———— and R. Lydekker, "Mammals Living and Extinct," A. & C. Black, London, 1891.

Frick, Hans, "Die Entwickling und Morphologie der Chrondrokraniums von Myotis," Verlag, Stuttgart.

Gladov, N. A., "The Flight of Birds," Moscow, 1949.

Goodwin, George G., "Mammals of Costa Rica," Bull. Am. Mus. Nat. Hist., 87, New York, 1946.

————, "Observations of Noctilio," Journ. Mammalogy, 9, 1928.

———— and Arthur M. Greenhall, "A Review of the Bats of Trinidad and Tobago," Bull. Am. Mus. Nat. Hist., Vol. 122, Art. 3, New York, 1961.

Greenhall, Arthur M., "The Food of Some Trinidad Fruit Bats," Journ. Agric. Soc., Trinidad and Tobago, 1956.

Grey, J. E., "Monkeys, Lemurs, and Fruit-eating Bats," British Museum (N.H.), 1870.

Griffin, Donald R., "Echoes of Bats and Men," Doubleday, New York, 1959.

————, "Listening in the Dark," Yale University Press, New Haven, 1958.

————, "Migrations of New England Bats," Bull. Mus. Comp. Zool., 86, Harvard University Press, 1940.

————, "Travels of Banded Cave Bats," Journ. Mammalogy, 26, 1945.

Hamilton, William J., Jr., "The Insect Food of the Big Brown Bat," Journ. Mammalogy, 14, 1933.

————, "The Mammals of the Eastern United States," Comstock, Ithaca, New York, 1943.

Hahn, W. L., "Some Habits and Sensory Adaptations of Cave-Inhabiting Bats," Biol. Bull., 15, 1908.

Handley, Charles O., Jr., "Review of American Bats of the Genera Euderma and Plecotus," Proc. U.S. Nat. Mus., Vol. 110, 1959.

Hitchcock, H. B. and K. Reynolds, "Homing Experiments with the Little Brown Bat, Myotis lucifugus l.," Journ. Mammalogy, 23, 1942.

Hopwood, A. Tyndall, "Lectures on the Development of Taxonomy," London, 1950.

Howell, A. H., "Notes on Diurnal Migrations of Bats," Proc. Biol. Soc., 21, Washington, 1908.

Husson, Antonius Marie, "The Bats of Suriname," Brill, Leiden, 1962.

International Code of Zoological Nomenclature, XV International Congress of Zoology, International Trust for Zoological Nomenclature, London, 1961.

Kuroda, Nagamichi, "A Monograph of the Japanese Mammals," Sanseido, Tokyo, 1940.

Laurie, Eleanor M. O. and J. E. Hill, "Land Mammals of New Guinea, Celebes and Adjacent Islands, 1758–1952." British Museum (N.H.), London, 1954.

Loveridge, Arthur, "Notes on East African Mammals," Proc. Zool. Soc., London, 1923.

Matschie, Paul, "Die Megachiroptera," des Berliner Museums für Naturkunde, Druck und Verlag von Georg Reimer, Berlin, 1899.

Matthew, W. D., "A Paleocene Bat," Bull. Am. Mus. Nat. Hist., 37, 1917.

————, "Climate and Evolution," Ann. N.Y. Acad. Sci., 1915.

Meise, Wilhelm, "Der Abendsegler," Geest und Portig, Leipzig, 1951.

Miller, Gerrit S., Jr., "The Families and Genera of Bats," Government Printing Office, Washington, 1907.

————, "Revision of the North American Bats of the Family Vespertilionidae," U.S. Dept. Agric., N.A. Fauna, 1897.

Miller, Gerrit S., Jr., and G. M. Allen, "The American Bats of the Genera *Myotis* and *Pizonyx*," U.S. Nat. Mus., Washington, 1928.

Mohr, Charles E., "Observations of the Young of Cave-dwelling Bats," *Journ. Mammalogy*, 14, 1933.

Ognev, S. I., "Mammals of the USSR and Adjacent Countries," Moscow, 1948.

Osborn, Henry Fairfield, "Evolution of Mammalian Molar Teeth," Macmillan, New York, 1907.

Peters, Wilhelm, "Über die Chiropterengottungen *Mormoops* und *Phyllostomae*," Berlin, 1857.

Ratcliffe, Francis N., "The Flying Fox (*Pteropus*) in Australia," *J. Anim. Ecology*, 1, 1932.

————, "Flying Foxes and Drifting Sand," Angus and Robertson, Sydney, 1948.

Raven, Henry C., "Wallace's Line and the Distribution of Indo-Australian Mammals," *Bull. Amer. Mus. Nat. Hist.*, Vol. LXVIII, 1935.

Ryberg, Olaf, "Studies on Bats and Bat Parasites," Bokförlaget Svensk Natur, Stockholm, 1947.

Schenk, E. T. and J. H. McMasters, "Procedure in Taxonomy," Stanford University Press, 1936.

Seton, E. T., "Story of Atalapha," *Scribner's Magazine*, 59, 1916.

Sharland, Michael, "Tasmanian Wildlife," Melbourne University Press, 1962.

Simpson, George Gaylord, "The Principles of Classification of Mammals," *Bull. Amer. Mus. Nat. Hist.*, 85, 1945.

Sperry, Charles G., "Opossum and Skunk Eat Bats," *Journ. Mammalogy*, 14, 1933.

Tate, G. H. H., "Molossid Bats of the Archbold Collections," *Am. Mus. Novitates*, Archbold 38, 1142, 1941.

————, "Review of the Genus *Hipposideros* with Special Reference to Indo-Australian Species," *Bull. Amer. Mus. Nat. Hist.*, Archbold 35, Vol. 78, Art. 5, 1941.

————, "Review of *Myotis* of Eurasia," *Bull. Am. Mus. Nat. Hist.*, Archbold 39, Vol. 78, Art. 8, 1941.

————, "Notes on Vespertilionid Bats of the Subfamilies *Miniopterinae, Murininae, Kerivoulinae* and *Nyctophilinae*," *Bull. Am. Mus. Nat. Hist.*, Archbold 40, Vol. 78, Art. 9, 1941.

————, "A New Genus and Species of Fruit Bats, Allied to *Nyctimene*," *Am. Mus. Novitates*, Archbold 46, 1204, 1942.

————, "Review of the Vespertilionine Bats, with Special Attention to Genera and Species of the Archbold Collections," *Bull. Am. Mus. Nat. Hist.*, Archbold 47, Vol. 80, Art. 7, 1942.

————, "*Pteropodidae* (Chiroptera) of the Archbold Collections," *Bull. Am. Mus. Nat. Hist.*, Archbold 48, Vol. 80, Art. 9, 1942.

————, "Further Notes on the *Rhinolophus philippinensis* Group (Chiroptera)," *Am. Mus. Novitates*, Archbold 49, No. 1219, 1943.

———— and Richard Archbold, "A Revision of the Genus *Emballonura* (Chiroptera)," *Am. Mus. Novitates*, Archbold 23, 1035, 1939.

———— and ————, "Oriental *Rhinolophus*, with Special Reference to Material from the Archbold Collections," *Am. Mus. Novitates*, Archbold 24, 1036, 1939.

Taylor, Edward H., "Philippine Land Mammals," Manila, 1934.

Trapido, Harold and Peter E. Crowe, "The Wing Banding Method in the Study of the Travels of Bats," *Journ. Mammalogy*, 27, 1946.

Trouessart, E. L., "Fauna des Mannifères d'Europe," Friedländer, Berlin, 1910.

Troughton, Ellis, "Furred Animals of Australia," Angus and Robertson, Sydney, 1941.

————, "Six New Bats (Microchiroptera) from the Australasian Region," *Aust. Zool.*, 8, 1937.

————, "The Habits and Food of Some Australian Mammals," *Aust. Zool.*, 7, 1931.

223

Van Gelder, Richard G., "Echolocation Failure in Migratory Bats," *Trans. Kansas Acad. Sci.*, 59, 1956.

Vesey-Fitzgerald, Brian, "British Bats," Methuen, London, 1949.

Wimsatt, William A., "Notes on Breeding Behavior, Pregnancy, and Parturition in Some Vespertilionid Bats of the Eastern United States," *Journ. Mammalogy*, 26, 1945.

———, "Survival of Spermatozoa in the Female Reproductive Tract of the Bat," *Anat. Rec.*, 83, 1942.

Winge, H., "The Relationships of the Mammalian Genera," C. A. Reitzels Forlag, Copenhagen, 1941.

Wood Jones, Frederic, "The Mammals of South Australia," British Scientific Guild, (S.A. branch), Adelaide, 1923.

Index

225

226